The Great Book of Real Madrid History and Trivia

Taft Johnson

The role of the book within our culture is changing. The change is brought on by new ways to acquire & use content, the rapid dissemination of information and real-time peer collaboration on a global scale. Despite these changes one thing is clear--"the book" in it's traditional form continues to play an important role in learning and communication. The book you are holding in your hands utilizes the unique characteristics of the Internet -- relying on web infrastructure and collaborative tools to share and use resources in keeping with the characteristics of the medium (user-created, defying control, etc.)--while maintaining all the convenience and utility of a real book.

Contents

Real Madrid C.F.

Full name	Real Madrid Club de Fútbol
Nickname(s)	*Los Blancos* (The Whites) *Los Merengues* (The Merengues)
Founded	March 6, 1902 as *Madrid Football Club*
Ground	Estadio Santiago Bernabéu, Madrid (Capacity: 80,354)
Honorary President	Alfredo Di Stéfano
President	Florentino Pérez
Head Coach	José Mourinho
League	La Liga
2009–10	La Liga, 2nd

Home colours	**Away colours**	**Third colours**
Current season		

Real Madrid Club de Fútbol (Spanish pronunciation: [reˈal maˈðrið ˈkluβ ðe ˈfutβol] *Royal Madrid Football Club*), commonly known as **Real Madrid**, is a professional association football club based in Madrid, Spain. It is the most successful team in Spanish football and was voted by FIFA as the most successful club of the 20th century, having won a record 31 La Liga titles, 17 Spanish "Copa del Rey" Cups, a record 9 UEFA Champions Leagues, 2 UEFA Cups, 1 UEFA Supercup, and 3 Intercontinental Cups. Real Madrid was a founding member of FIFA and the now-defunct G–14 group of Europe's leading football clubs as well as its replacement, the European Club Association. The word "Real" in the club's name is the Spanish term for "royal", and was given by the King Alfonso XIII in 1920 together with the royal crown in the emblem – several other Spanish football teams also received this royal distinction: Real Sociedad, Real Unión de Irún, Real Betis, and Real Zaragoza.

Founded in 1902, Real Madrid never relegated from La Liga, the top league of Spanish football. The club established itself as a major force in both Spanish and European football during the 1950s. In the 1980s, the club had one of the best teams (known as *La Quinta del Buitre*) in Spain and Europe, winning two UEFA Cups, five consecutive Spanish championships, one Spanish Cup and three Spanish Super Cups.

The team's traditional home kit colour is white, although it initially adopted a blue oblique stripe on the shirt. Its crest has been changed several times in attempts to modernise or re-brand it. The current crest is a modified version of the one first adopted in the 1920s. Real Madrid's home ground is the 80,354-seater Santiago Bernabéu football stadium in downtown Madrid, where it has played since 1947. In 2010 the Bernabéu held the final of the UEFA Champions League.

Real Madrid holds long-standing rivalries with other football clubs, most notably FC Barcelona, with matches between the two teams referred to as "el Clásico". Unlike most European football clubs, Real Madrid's members (*socios*) have owned and operated the club since its inception. The club is the world's richest football club (€401m) in terms of revenue and the second most valuable hencing over €950m in 2008.

History

Main article: History of Real Madrid C.F.

Early years, Civil War and Franco (1902–1945)

Real Madrid's origins go back to when football was introduced to Madrid by the academics and students of the *Institución libre de enseñanza*, which included several Oxbridge graduates. They founded *Football Club Sky* in 1897, playing on Sunday mornings at Moncloa. It split into two clubs in 1900: *New Foot-Ball de Madrid* and Club Español de Madrid. The latter club split again in 1902, resulting in the formation of *Real Madrid Football Club* on 6 March 1902. Three years after its foundation, in 1905, *Madrid FC* won its first title after defeating Athletic Bilbao in the Spanish Cup final. The club became one of the founding sides of the Royal Spanish Football Federation on 4 January 1909, when club president Adolfo Meléndez signed the foundation agreement of the Spanish FA. After moving between grounds the team moved to the *Campo de O'Donnell* in 1912. In 1920, the club's name was changed to Real Madrid after King Alfonso XIII granted the title of Real (Royal) to the club.

In 1929, the first Spanish football league was founded. Real Madrid led the first league season until the last match, a loss to Athletic Bilbao, meant they finished runners-up to Barcelona. Real Madrid won its first League title in the 1931–32 season. Real won the League again the following year, becoming the first side to have won the championship twice.

Santiago Bernabéu Yeste and European success (1945–1978)

Santiago Bernabéu Yeste became president of Real Madrid in 1945. Under his presidency, the club, its stadium Santiago Bernabéu and its training facilities Ciudad Deportiva were rebulit after the Spanish Civil War damages. Beginning in 1953, he embarked upon a strategy of signing world-class players from abroad, the most prominent of them being Alfredo Di Stéfano.

In 1955, acting upon the idea proposed by the French sports journalist and editor of *L'Équipe* Gabriel Hanot, Bernabéu, Bedrignan and Gusztáv Sebes created an exhibition tournament of invited teams from around Europe that would eventually become what today is known as the UEFA Champions League. It was under Bernabéu's guidance that Real Madrid established itself as a major force in both Spanish and European football. The club won the European Cup five times in a row between 1956 and 1960, which included the 7–3 Hampden Park final against Eintracht Frankfurt in 1960. After these five consecutive successes, Real was permanently awarded the original cup and earning the right to wear the UEFA badge of honour. The club won the European Cup for a sixth time in 1966 defeating FK Partizan 2–1 in the final with a team composed entirely of same nationality players, a first in the competition. This team became known as the "Ye-yé". The name "Ye-yé" came from the "Yeah, yeah, yeah" chorus in the Beatles' song "She Loves You" after four members of the team posed for *Diario Marca* dressed in Beatles wigs. The Ye-yé generation was also European Cup runner-up in 1962 and 1964.

In the 1970s, Real Madrid won 5 league championships and 3 Spanish Cups. The club played its first UEFA Cup Winners' Cup final in 1971 and lost to English side Chelsea 2–1. On 2 July 1978, club president Santiago Bernabéu died while the World Cup was being played in Argentina. The International Federation of Association Football (FIFA) decreed three days of mourning to honour him during the tournament. The following year, the club organized the first edition of the Santiago Bernabéu Trophy in the memory of its former president.

Quinta del Buitre and seventh European Cup (1980s–2000)

By the early 1980s, Real Madrid had lost its grasp on the La Liga title until a new batch of home-grown stars brought domestic success back to the club. Spanish sport journalist Julio César Iglesias gave to this generation the name *La Quinta del Buitre* ("Vulture's Cohort"), which was derived from the nickname given to one of its members, Emilio Butragueño. The other four members were Manuel Sanchís, Martín Vázquez, Míchel and Miguel Pardeza. With *La Quinta del Buitre* (reduced to four members when Pardeza left the club for Zaragoza in 1986) and notable players like goalkeeper Francisco Buyo, right-back Miguel Porlán *Chendo* and Mexican striker Hugo Sánchez, Real Madrid had one of the best teams in Spain and Europe during the second half of the 1980s, winning two UEFA Cups, five Spanish championships in a row, one Spanish cup and three Spanish Super Cups. In the early 1990s, *La Quinta del Buitre* split up after Martín Vázquez, Emilio Butragueño and Míchel left the club.

In 1996, President Lorenzo Sanz appointed Fabio Capello as coach. Although his tenure lasted only one season, Real Madrid was proclaimed league champion and players like Roberto Carlos, Predrag Mijatović, Davor Šuker and Clarence Seedorf arrived at the club to strengthen a squad that already boasted the likes of Raúl, Fernando Hierro, Iván Zamorano, and Fernando Redondo. As a result, Real Madrid (with the addition of Fernando Morientes in 1997) finally ended its 32-year wait for its seventh European Cup. In 1998, under manager Jupp Heynckes, The Whites defeated Juventus 1–0 in the final thanks to a goal from Predrag Mijatović.

Los Galácticos, Calderón and second Pérez era (2000–present)

In July 2000, Florentino Pérez was elected club president. He vowed in his campaign to erase the club's debt and modernize the club's facilities. However, the primary electoral promise that propelled Pérez to victory was the signing of Luís Figo. The following year, the club got its training ground rezoned and used the money to begin assembling the famous *Galáctico* side including players such as Zinédine Zidane, Ronaldo, Luís Figo, Roberto Carlos, Raúl and David Beckham. It is debatable whether the gamble paid off, as despite a European Cup win in 2002, followed by the League in 2003, the club failed to win a major trophy for the next three seasons.

Ramón Calderón was elected as club president on 2 July 2006 and subsequently appointed Fabio Capello as the new coach and Predrag Mijatović as the new sporting director. Real Madrid won the La Liga title in 2007 for the first time in four years but Capello was sacked. In the 2007–08 season, The Whites won the domestic league for the 31st time, achieving their first consecutive league title in eighteen years. On 1 June 2009, Florentino Pérez regained Real Madrid's presidency. Pérez continued with the *Galácticos* policy pursued in his first term, buying Kaká from A.C. Milan then purchasing Cristiano Ronaldo from Manchester United for a record breaking £80 million.

Crest and colours

Real Madrid's original kit

The first crest had a simple design consisting of a decorative interlacing of the three initials of the club, "MCF" for Madrid Club de Fútbol, in dark blue on a white shirt. The first change in the crest occurred in 1908 when the letters adopted a more streamlined form and appeared inside a circle. The next change in the configuration of the crest did not occur until the presidency of Pedro Parages in 1920. At that time, King Alfonso XIII granted the club his royal patronage which came in the form of the title "Real madrid", roughly translated as "Royal". Thus, Alfonso's crown was added to the crest and the club styled itself *Real Madrid Club de Fútbol*. With the dissolution of the monarchy in 1931, all the royal symbols (the crown on the crest and the title of Real) were eliminated. The crown was replaced by the dark mulberry band of the Region of Castile. In 1941, two years after the end of the Civil War, the crest's "Real Corona", or "Royal Crown", was restored while the mulberry stripe of Castile was retained as well. In addition, the whole crest was made full color, with gold being the most prominent, and the club was again called Real Madrid Club de Fútbol. The most recent modification to the crest occurred in 2001 when the club wanted to better situate itself for the twenty-first century and further standardize its crest. One of the modifications made was changing the mulberry stripe to a more bluish shade.

Real Madrid's traditional home colours are all white, although it initially adopted a blue oblique stripe on the shirt (the design was kept in the club crest); but unlike today, dark blue socks were worn. The striped shirt was replaced by an all-white version, modeled after the shirt worn by Corinthian F.C., in 1902. In the same year, the blue socks were replaced by black ones. By the early 1940s the manager changed the kit again by adding buttons to the shirt and the club's crest on the left breast (which have remained ever since). On 23 November 1947, in a game against Atlético Madrid at the *Metropolitano* Stadium, Real Madrid became the first Spanish team to wear numbered shirts.

Real's traditional away colours are all black or all purple. The club's kit is currently manufactured by Adidas whose contract extends from 1998. Real Madrid's first shirt sponsor, Zanussi, agreed for the 1982–83, 1983–84 and 1984–85 seasons. Following that, the club was sponsored by Parmalat and Otaysa before a long-term deal was signed with Teka in 1992. In 2001, Real Madrid ended their contract with Teka and for one season used the Realmadrid.com logo to promote the club's website. Then, in 2002, a deal was signed with Siemens Mobile and in 2006, the BenQ Siemens logo appeared on the club's shirt. Real Madrid's current shirt sponsor is bwin.com following the economic problems of BenQ Siemens.

Stadium

Main articles: Santiago Bernabéu Stadium, Alfredo Di Stéfano Stadium, and Estadio Chamartín

Real Madrid at Santiago Bernabéu during a 2007 match with Real Betis

After moving between grounds the team moved to the *"Campo de O'Donnell"* in 1912, which remained its home ground for eleven years. After this period, the club moved for one year to the *Campo de Ciudad Lineal*, a small ground with a capacity of 8,000 spectators. After that, Real Madrid moved its home matches to *Estadio Chamartín* which was inaugurated on 17 May 1923 with a match against Newcastle United. In this stadium, which hosted 22,500 spectators, Real Madrid celebrated its first Spanish league title. After some successes, the 1943 elected president Santiago Bernabéu decided that the

Estadio Chamartín was not big enough for the ambitions of the club. A new stadium was built and was inaugurated on 14 December 1947. This was the Santiago Bernabéu Stadium as it is known today, although it did not acquire this name until 1955. The first match held on Bernabéu was played between Real Madrid and the Portuguese club Belenenses and won by The Whites with 3–1, the first goal being scored by Sabino Barinaga.

The capacity has changed frequently, peaking at 120,000 after a 1953 expansion. Since then, there have been a number of reductions due to modernizations (the last standing places went away in 1998–99 in response to UEFA regulations which forbids standing at matches in the UEFA competition), countered to some extent by expansions. The last change was an increase of about five thousand to a capacity of 80,354, effected in 2003. A plan to add a retractable roof has been announced.

The Bernabéu has hosted the 1964 European Championship final, the 1982 FIFA World Cup final, the 1957, 1969 and 1980 European Cup finals and the 2010 Champions League Final. The stadium has its own Madrid Metro station along the 10 line called *Santiago Bernabéu*. On 14 November 2007, the Bernabéu has been upgraded to Elite Football Stadium status by UEFA.

On 9 May 2006, the Alfredo Di Stéfano Stadium was inaugurated at the City of Madrid where Real Madrid usually trains. The inaugural match was played between Real Madrid and Stade Reims, a rematch of the 1956 European Cup final. Real Madrid won the match 6–1 with goals from Sergio Ramos, Cassano (2), Soldado (2), and Jurado. The venue is now part of the Ciudad Real Madrid, the club's new training facilities located outside Madrid in Valdebebas. The stadium holds 5,000 people and is Real Madrid Castilla's home ground. It is named after former Real footballer Alfredo Di Stéfano.

Statistics and records

Main article: List of Real Madrid C.F. records and statistics

Raúl is Real Madrid's all-time top goalscorer and top appearance.

Raúl holds the record for most Real Madrid appearances, having played 741 first-team matches from 1994 to 2010. Manuel Sanchis, Jr. comes second, having played 711 times. The record for a goalkeeper is held by Iker Casillas, with 518 appearances. With 127 caps (47 while at the club), Luís Figo of Portugal is Real's most capped international player.

Raúl is Real's all-time top goalscorer, with 323 goals in 741 games (1994–2010). Four other players have also scored over 200 goals for Real: Alfredo Di Stefano (1953–64), Santillana (1971–88), Ferenc Puskás (1958–66) and Hugo Sánchez (1985–92). Sánchez holds the record for the most league goals scored in one season (38 in 1989–90). Di Stéfano's 49 goals in 58 matches was for decades the all-time highest tally in the European Cup, until it was surpassed by Raúl in 2005. The fastest goal in the history of the club (15 seconds) was scored by Brazilian Ronaldo on 3 December 2003 during a league match against Atlético Madrid.

Officially, the highest home attendance figure for a Real Madrid match is 83,329, which was for a football cup competition, Copa del Rey, in 2006. The current legal capacity of Estadio Santiago Bernabeu is 80,354. The club's average attendance in 2007–08 season was 76,234, the highest in European Leagues. Real has also set records in Spanish football, most notably the most domestic titles (31 as of 2007–08) and the most seasons won in a row (5, during 1960–65 and 1985–90). With 121 matches (from 17 February 1957 to 7 March 1965), the club holds the record for longest unbeaten run at home in La Liga.

The Whites also hold the record for winning the UEFA Champions League nine times and for the most semi-final appearances (21). Raúl González is the all-time UEFA Champions League top scorer, with 66 goals. The team has the record number of consecutive participation in the European Cup with 15, from 1955–56 to 1969–70.

In June 2009, the club broke its own record for the highest transfer fee ever paid in the history of football by agreeing to pay Manchester United €96 million ($131.5 million, £80 million) for the services of Cristiano Ronaldo. The fee of €76 million (over $100 million, £45.8 million) for Zinedine Zidane's transfer from Juventus to Real Madrid in 2001 was the previous highest transfer fee ever paid. In June 2009, Real Madrid also agreed to buy Kaká from AC Milan for a fee that broke the previous record in pounds sterling. The club's record sale came on 1 September 2008, when they sold Robinho to Manchester City for €42 million (£32.5 million).

Support

During most home matches the majority of the seats in the stadium are occupied by season ticket holders, of which there are average of 68,670. To become a season ticket holder one must first be a *socio*, or club member. In addition to members, the club has more than 1,800 *peñas* (official, club-affiliated supporters' groups) in Spain and around the world. Real Madrid has the highest average all-time attendance in Spanish football and regularly attracts over 65,000 fans to Santiago Bernabéu; it was the second best-supported La Liga team in the 2004–05 season, with an average gate of 71,900. Real Madrid's hardcore supporters are the so-called *Ultras Sur* supporters. They are known for their extreme right-wing politics. The Ultras Sur have developed an alliance with other right wing groups, most notably S.S. Lazio *Irriducibili* fans. On several occasions they have racially abused opposing players, and have been investigated by UEFA for doing so.

Rivalries

El Clásico

Main article: El Clásico

There is often a fierce rivalry between the two strongest teams in a national league, and this is particularly the case in La Liga, where the game between Real Madrid and FC Barcelona is known as 'The Classic' (*El Clásico*). From the start of national competitions the clubs were seen as representatives of two rival regions in Spain: Catalonia and Castile, as well as of the two cities. The rivalry reflects what many regard as the political and cultural tensions felt between Catalans and the Castilians, seen by one author as a re-enactment of the Spanish Civil War.

During the dictatorships of Primo de Rivera and especially of Francisco Franco (1939–1975), all regional cultures were suppressed. All of the languages spoken in Spanish territory, except Spanish (Castilian) itself, were officially banned. Symbolising the Catalan people's desire for freedom, FC Barcelona became 'More than a club' (*Més que un club*) for the Catalans. According to Manuel Vázquez Montalbán, the best way for the Catalans to demonstrate their identity was by joining FC Barcelona. It was less risky than joining a clandestine anti-Franco movement, and allowed them to express their dissidence.

On the other hand, Real Madrid was widely seen as the embodiment of the sovereign oppressive centralism and the fascist regime at management level and beyond (Santiago Bernabeu, the former club president for whom the Merengues stadium is named, fought with *los nacionales*). However, during the Spanish Civil War, members of both clubs such as Josep Sunyol and Rafael Sánchez Guerra suffered at the hands of Franco supporters.

During the 1950s the rivalry was exacerbated further when there was a controversy surrounding the transfer of Alfredo di Stéfano, who finally played for Real Madrid and was key to their subsequent success. The 1960s saw the rivalry reach the European stage when they met twice at the knock-out rounds of the European Cup. The latest European encounter between the clubs, in 2002, was dubbed the "Match of The Century" by Spanish media, and was watched by more than 500 million people.

El Derbi madrileño

Main article: El Derbi madrileño

The club's nearest neighbour is Atlético Madrid, a rivalry being shared between fans of both football teams. Although Atlético was originally founded by three Basque students in 1903, it was joined in 1904 by dissident members of *Madrid FC*. Further tensions came because initially Real supporters came from the middle class while the Atlético supporters were drawn from the working class. Today these distinctions are largely blurred. They met for the first time on 21 February 1929 in matchday three of the first League Championship at the former Chamartín. It was the first official derby of the new tournament, and Real won 2–1. The rivalry first gained international attention in 1959 during the European Cup when the two clubs met in the semi-final. Real won the first leg 2–1 at the Bernabéu while Atlético won 1–0 at the *Metropolitano*. The tie went to a replay and The Whites won 2–1. Atlético, however, gained some revenge when, led by former Real Madrid coach José Villalonga, it defeated The Whites in two successive *Copa del Generalísimo* finals in 1960 and 1961.

Between 1961 and 1989, when Real dominated La Liga, only Atlético offered it any serious challenge, winning Liga titles in 1966, 1970, 1973 and 1977. In 1965, Atlético became the first team to beat Real at the Bernabéu in eight years. Real Madrid's record against Atlético in more recent times is very favorable. A high point coming in the 2002–03 season, when The Whites clinched the La Liga title after an impressive victory at Atlético 0–4 at the Vicente Calderón Stadium.

Finances and ownership

In 2010, *Forbes* evaluated Real Madrid's worth to be around €992 million (USD $1,323 million), ranking them second after Manchester United, based on figures from the 2008–09 season. According to Deloitte, Real Madrid had a recorded revenue of €401 million in the same period, ranking first.

Along with FC Barcelona, Athletic Bilbao, and Osasuna, Real Madrid is organised as a registered association. Unlike a limited company, it is not possible to purchase shares in the club, but only membership. The members of Real Madrid, called *socios*, form an assembly of delegates which is the highest governing body of the club. As of 2010 the club has 60,000 *socios*.

At the end of the 2009–10 season, the club board of directories stated that Real Madrid had a net debt of €244.6 million, 82.1 million lower than the previous fiscal year.

Popular culture

Real Madrid was the featured club in the second edition of the *Goal!* football movie trilogy, *Goal! 2: Living the Dream...* (2007). The film follows former Newcastle United star Santiago Muñez as he is first scouted, and then signed by Real Madrid for the 2005–06 season. The film's creators wanted to put emphasis on the changes in Muñez's life after his move to Madrid. Production was done with the full support of UEFA, allowing the film crew to use many real life players in cameo roles. Real Madrid squad members featured in the film included Iker Casillas, Zinedine Zidane, David Beckham, Ronaldo, Roberto Carlos, Raúl, Sergio Ramos, Robinho, Thomas Gravesen, Michael Owen, Míchel Salgado, Júlio Baptista, Steve McManaman, Jonathan Woodgate, and Iván Helguera. Non-Real Madrid players to make cameo appearances included Ronaldinho, Thierry Henry, Lionel Messi, Samuel Eto'o, Andrés Iniesta, Pablo Aimar, Fredrik Ljungberg, Cesc Fàbregas, Santiago Cañizares and others. In the film, both Florentino Pérez and Alfredo Di Stéfano presented the fictional player Muñez to the club after his signing.

Real, The Movie is a 2005 part feature, part documentary film that showcases the world-wide passion for Real Madrid C.F. Produced by the club and directed by Borja Manso, it follows five sub-stories of fans from around the world and their love for Real Madrid. Along with the fictional portion of the film, it also contains real footage of the squad, during training at Ciudad Real Madrid, matches, and interviews. Although the film mentions all of the squad, it mainly focuses on Los Galácticos such as David Beckham, Zinedine Zidane, Raúl, Luís Figo, Ronaldo, Iker Casillas, and Roberto Carlos, among others. The film was originally produced in Spanish, but has been dubbed for their world-wide fanbase.

The book *White Storm: 100 years of Real Madrid* by Phil Ball was the first English-language history of Real Madrid. Published in 2002, it talks about the most successful moments of the club during its first centenary, having been translated into various languages.

Players

Main article: List of Real Madrid C.F. players

Spanish teams are limited to three players without EU citizenship. The squad list includes only the principal nationality of each player; several non-European players on the squad have dual citizenship with an EU country. Also, players from the ACP countries—countries in Africa, the Caribbean, and the Pacific that are signatories to the Cotonou Agreement—are not counted against non-EU quotas due to the Kolpak ruling.

Current squad

As of 14 September 2010

Note: Flags indicate national team as has been defined under FIFA eligibility rules. Players may hold more than one non-FIFA nationality.

No.	Position	Player
1	GK	Iker Casillas *(captain)*
2	DF	Ricardo Carvalho
3	DF	Pepe
4	DF	Sergio Ramos *(vice captain)*
5	MF	Fernando Gago
6	MF	Mahamadou Diarra
7	FW	Cristiano Ronaldo
8	MF	Kaká
9	FW	Karim Benzema
10	MF	Lassana Diarra
11	MF	Esteban Granero
12	DF	Marcelo
13	GK	Antonio Adán
14	MF	Xabi Alonso
15	DF	David Mateos
16	MF	Sergio Canales
17	DF	Álvaro Arbeloa
18	DF	Raúl Albiol
19	DF	Ezequiel Garay
20	FW	Gonzalo Higuaín
21	MF	Pedro León
22	MF	Ángel di María
23	MF	Mesut Özil

24		MF	Sami Khedira
25		GK	Jerzy Dudek

Out on loan

Note: Flags indicate national team as has been defined under FIFA eligibility rules. Players may hold more than one non-FIFA nationality.

No.		Position	Player
—		MF	Royston Drenthe *(to Hércules CF)*

Personnel

Current technical staff

See also List of Real Madrid C.F. managers

Position	Staff
Head coach	José Mourinho
Assistant Coach	Aitor Karanka
Fitness Trainer	Rui Faria
Goalkeeper Coach	Silvino Louro
Technical Assistant	José Morais

Last updated: 22 September 2010

Source: Real Madrid [1]

Management

See also: List of Real Madrid C.F. presidents

Businessman Florentino Pérez is the current president of the club.

Office	Name
President	Florentino Pérez
Honorary Life President	Alfredo Di Stéfano
1st Vice-president	Fernando Fernández Tapias
2nd Vice-president	Eduardo Fernández de Blas
Board secretary	Enrique Sánchez González
General Director	Jorge Valdano
General Diretor of President's Office	Manuel Redondo
Director of Institutional Relations	Emilio Butragueño
Advisor to the President	Zinedine Zidane
Sporting Director	Miguel Pardeza
Director of the Social Area	José Luis Sánchez
Director of the Legal Advisory Board	Javier López Farre

Last updated: 1 July 2010

Source: Real Madrid [2]

Honours

Historically, Real Madrid is Spain's most successful team, having won 57 domestic trophies, and one of the most recognized football clubs in the world, having won 15 international trophies, making them the second most successful team in Europe and third in the world for official international competition won, all recognized by UEFA and FIFA; it also has the record in La Liga titles (with 31) and European Cup/UEFA Champions League titles (with 9). The club was placed first in the FIFA Clubs of the 20th Century's selection on 23 December 2000. It also received the FIFA Order of Merit in 2004. Added to this, Real is allowed to wear a multiple-winner badge on their shirt during UEFA Champions League matches as they have won more than five European Cups.

Domestic

- **La Liga**

  Winners (31): 1931–32, 1932–33, 1953–54, 1954–55, 1956–57, 1957–58, 1960–61, 1961–62, 1962–63, 1963–64, 1964–65, 1966–67, 1967–68, 1968–69, 1971–72, 1974–75, 1975–76, 1977–78, 1978–79, 1979–80, 1985–86, 1986–87, 1987–88, 1988–89, 1989–90, 1994–95, 1996–97, 2000–01, 2002–03, 2006–07, 2007–08

  Runners-up (19): 1928–29, 1933–34, 1934–35, 1935–36, 1941–42, 1944–45, 1958–59, 1959–60, 1965–66, 1980–81, 1982–83, 1983–84, 1991–92, 1992–93, 1998–99, 2004–05, 2005–06, 2008–09, 2009–10

- **Copa del Rey**

  Winners (17): 1905, 1906, 1907, 1908, 1917, 1934, 1936, 1946, 1947, 1962, 1970, 1974, 1975, 1979–80, 1981–82, 1988–89, 1992–93

  Runners-up (19): 1903, 1916, 1918, 1924, 1929, 1930, 1933, 1940, 1943, 1958, 1960, 1961, 1968, 1978–79, 1982–83, 1989–90, 1991–92, 2001–02, 2003–04

- **Supercopa de España**

  Winners (8): 1988, 1989*, 1990, 1993, 1997, 2001, 2003, 2008

  Runners-up (3): 1982, 1995, 2007

  (Won Copa del Rey and La Liga)*

- **Copa de la Liga**

  Winners (1): 1984–85

  Runners-up (1): 1982–83

European

- **European Cup/ UEFA Champions League**

  Winners (9): 1955–56*, 1956–57, 1957–58, 1958–59, 1959–60, 1965–66, 1997–98, 1999–2000, 2001–02

  Runners-up (3): 1961–62, 1963–64, 1980–81

  (* *First ever winners*)

- **UEFA Cup/ UEFA Europa League**

  Winners (2): 1984–85, 1985–86

- **UEFA Cup Winners' Cup**

  Runners-up (2): 1970–71, 1982–83

- **UEFA Super Cup**

  Winners (1): 2002

  Runners-up (2): 1998, 2000

- **Latin Cup**

  Winners (2): 1955, 1957

- **Copa Iberoamericana**

  Winners (1): 1994

Worldwide

- **Intercontinental Cup/ FIFA Club World Cup**

  Winners (3): 1960, 1998, 2002

  Runners-up (2): 1966, 2000

See also

Sports

- Real Madrid Baloncesto

Reserve teams

- Real Madrid Castilla
- Real Madrid C

Other

- Trofeo Santiago Bernabéu
- List of fan-owned sports teams
- Richest football clubs

External links

Official websites

- Realmadrid.com [3] Official club website (Spanish) / (English) / (Japanese) / (Arabic)
- Real Madrid, Canal Oficial [4] YouTube's official Real Madrid channel
- Real Madrid Club de Fútbol [5] at the Liga de Fútbol Profesional official website (Spanish)
- Real Madrid CF [6] at the UEFA official website

News sites

- Real Madrid news [7] from Marca (Spanish)
- Real Madrid news [8] from AS (Spanish)
- Real Madrid news [9] from Sky Sports
- ESPN Real Madrid page [10]

References

Sources

- Dénes, Tamás & Rochy, Zoltán (2002). *Real Madrid.* Aréna 2000. ISBN 963-86167-5-X.
- Ball, Phil (2003 New edition). *Morbo: The Story of Spanish Football.* WSC Books Limited. ISBN 0-954-01346-8.
- Ball, Phil (2003). *White Storm: The Story of Real Madrid.* Mainstream. ISBN 1-84018-763-8.
- McManaman, Steve & Edworthy, Sarah (2003). *El Macca: Four Years with Real Madrid.* Simon & Schuster. ISBN 0-743-48920-9.
- Luis Miguel González, Luis González López, Fundación Real Madrid (2002). *Real Madrid: Cien años de leyenda, 1902–2002.* Everest. ISBN 84-241-9215-X.

Notes

ckb:دیرد□م لای□

History of Real Madrid C.F.

This article is about the **history of Real Madrid C.F.**, a football club based in Madrid, Spain. For an overview of the club, see Real Madrid C.F.

Early years

Football was introduced to Madrid by the professors and students of the *Institución Libre de Enseñanza*. They included several Oxbridge graduates. In 1895 they founded the club *Football Sky*, playing on Sunday mornings at Moncloa. In 1900 this club split into two different clubs *New Foot-Ball de Madrid* and Club Español de Madrid. The president of the latter club was Julián Palacios. In 1902 the latter club split again, resulting in the formation of *Sociedad Madrid FC* on March 6, 1902. The first president was Juan Padrós Rubió; the first secretary was *Manuel Mendía*; and the first treasurer was *José de Gorostizaga*. Juan Padrós Rubió would be later succeeded by his brother, Carlos Padrós from Spain. In 1905, only three years after its foundation, *Madrid FC* already won its first major title in the Estadio Chamartín stadium. The team won the first of four consecutive Copa del Rey - titles (at that time the only statewide competition). In 1912 they moved to their first ground called **'Campo de O'Donnell'** after moving between some minor grounds. In 1920 the club's name was changed into *Real Madrid* after King Alfonso XIII, a reputed football fan, granted the title of *Real* (Royal) to the club. However, when the Second Spanish Republic was proclaimed the club dropped both the word *Real* and the royal crown from the emblem, being known from then and until the end of the Spanish Civil War as *Madrid C. F.* only. The addition of the purple band to the emblem dates back to the Republican period and has remained there since then. In 1937, due to the stagnation of the ongoing civil war, all activity disappeared and the club virtually ceased to exist.

Real Madrid team in 1905

Santiago Bernabéu Yeste

Before becoming President in 1945, Santiago Bernabéu Yeste had already carried out the functions of player, first-team captain, club maintenance, first-team manager and director, in an association with the club that lasted nearly 70 years. He was responsible for rebuilding the club after the Spanish Civil War, and under his presidency, the Santiago Bernabéu Stadium and the Ciudad Deportiva. Real Madrid has a newly named stadium which is the Alfredo di Stéfano Stadium.

He also reorganized the club at all levels, in what would become the normal operating hierarchy of professional clubs in the future, giving every section and level of the club independent technical teams and recruiting staff such as Raimundo Saporta.

Finally, beginning in 1953 he embarked upon a strategy of signing world-class players from abroad, the most prominent of them being the signing of Alfredo di Stéfano and built the world's first truly multinational side. During Bernabéu's presidency many of Real Madrid's most legendary names played for the club, including the aforementioned Alfredo Di Stéfano, Ferenc Puskás, Francisco Gento, Héctor Rial, Raymond Kopa, José Santamaría, Miguel Muñoz, Amancio, Santillana. Under the administration of UEFA, it is the world's premier club tournament.

It was under Bernabéu's guidance, that Real Madrid became established as a major force in both Spanish and European football. Before passing away in 1978, Bernabéu had been the club's president for 33 years, during which he won 1 Intercontinental Cup, 6 European Cups, 16 La Liga titles, and 6 Spanish Cups.

International success

Araquistáin
Pachín
de Felipe
Zoco
Martínez
Pirri
Velázquez
Serena
Amaro
Grosso
Gento (C)

1966 European Cup Final starting lineup.

Alonso
Atienza
Marquitos
Lesmes
Muñoz (C)
Zárraga
Fernández
Ribó
Di Stéfano
Rial
Gento
1956 European Cup Final starting lineup.

In addition to their domestic success, Real Madrid's reputation as a major club was established by their outstanding record in the European Cup. To date they have been crowned champions of Europe a record nine times. Alfredo Di Stéfano, Ferenc Puskás and other famous players helped the club win the European Cup five times in a row between 1956 and 1960, which included the memorable 7-3 Hampden Park final against Eintracht Frankfurt in 1960. The club won for a sixth time in 1966 with the team known as the Ye-Ye , defeating Partizan Belgrade 2-1 in the final with a team composed entirely of nationally-born players, a first in the competition. They were also runners-up in 1962, 1964 and 1981. Winning the competition five consecutive times saw Real permanently awarded the original cup and earning the right to wear the UEFA badge of honour. They have also won the UEFA Cup twice and were twice runners-up in the European Cup Winners Cup.

In 1996 President Lorenzo Sanz appointed Fabio Capello as coach. Although his tenure lasted only one season, Real Madrid were proclaimed league champions and several important players arrived at the club (Roberto Carlos, Predrag Mijatović, Davor Šuker and Clarence Seedorf) to strengthen a squad that already boasted the likes of Raúl, Fernando Hierro and Fernando Redondo. As a result, Real Madrid (with the addition of Fernando Morientes in 1997) finally ended its 32-year wait for the seventh European Cup in 1998 under manager Jupp Heynckes, defeating Juventus 1-0 in the final, thanks to a goal from Predrag Mijatović. Real Madrid would go on to win again in 2000 and 2002 under manager Vicente Del Bosque, with sides including players such as Luís Figo and Zinedine Zidane.

Real Madrid is also three-time winners of the Intercontinental Cup, defeating Peñarol, Vasco da Gama, and Olimpia Asunción in 1960, 1998, and 2002 respectively.

The Luis de Carlos Era (1978-1985)

After a brief period as interim President, Raimundo Saporta called for elections. The Club's treasurer, Luis de Carlos, resigned in order to run for President. 26 July 1978 was the deadline for candidates to apply in order to run for office. De Carlos submitted 3,352 documents endorsing his candidacy, while the rest -gynaecologist Campos Gil and florist José Daguerre- didn't get the minimum number required in time. This called off the election and Luis de Carlos was proclaimed President of Real Madrid.

On 4 June 1980, the Santiago Bernabéu hosted the Cup final between Real Madrid and Castilla, the Club's second team, created on 21 July 1972. Castilla managed to defeat four First Division teams -Hércules, Athletic Bilbao, Real Sociedad and Sporting Gijon- to get to the final of the Spanish Championship. Real Madrid defeated Castilla -coached by the sorely missed Juanjo- 6-1.

France Football named Real Madrid the Best European Team of 1980. The jury took into account the two national titles the team won that year -the League and the King's Cup- and the fact that they reached the semifinals of the European Cup that season.

The 1980/81 season had an unpleasant finish for Madrid. On 26 April 1981, they lost the League when the victory chant was already being sung in Valladolid. Real Sociedad, who drew (2-2) against Sporting in the last minute at El Molinón claimed the title. Barely one month later, on 27 May, an Alan Kennedy goal (82nd minute) gave Liverpool the European Cup.

The professional Real Madrid squad was one of four teams of the Primera Division to back the strike called on 11 April 1982. On that day, the Whites played at Castellón with Castilla footballers and defeated the hosts 2-1.

The final of the 1982 World Cup took place at the Santiago Bernabéu Stadium. In a thrilling match, Italy outplayed Germany and won 3-1. What most spectators will remember most from that 11 July 1982 was the joy that overcame Sandro Pertini, President if Italy, each time the Italian side scored.

With the Presidential elections on the horizon, candidate Luis de Carlos introduced Alfredo di Stéfano and Amancio Amaro as coaches of the first team and Castilla on 19 May 1982. The Arrow left Madrid in 1964 and returned to the Club 18 years later. De Carlos defeated Ramón Mendoza in the election and Di Stéfano, who signed on for two years, won five runners-up titles in his first year as the Madridista coach.

Once the 1983/84 season had ended, Alfredo di Stéfano again said goodbye to Real Madrid. Twenty-one years later he went through the same experience. His contract ended on 30 June 1984 and Luis de Carlos decided not to resign him due to the failure to achieve sporting success.

On 12 December 1984, Emilio Butragueño became a European household name with an unforgettable performance against Anderlecht at the Bernabéu. The Belgians were coming off a 3-0 first leg win in Brussels and had the next round of the UEFA Cup in sight, but Butragueño crushed all their hopes with three goals (the other three were scored by Valdano, two, and Sanchís) and Real Madrid won convincingly 6-1.

After two brief stints as a Director and an election-time defeat to Luis de Carlos, Ramón Mendoza's became President of Real Madrid in 1985. Mendoza's arrival was the dawn of a new era in the history of the Club.

Real Madrid's first two UEFA Cup titles were won back-to-back. The first in 1984 against Hungary's Videoton (3-0 at Sosto Stadium and 0-1 in Chamartín), and the second one year later after defeating FC Köln 5-1 at the Bernabéu and losing 2-0 at the Olympiastadion in Berlin.

The Ramón Mendoza Era (1985-1995)

For more details on this topic, see Quinta del Buitre

Quinta del Buitre was the name given to the generation of club grown Real Madrid players that dominated Spanish football in the 1980s. The name ("Vulture's Cohort") was derived from the nickname given to its most charismatic member Emilio Butragueño. The other four members were Manolo Sanchís, Martín Vázquez, Míchel and Miguel Pardeza.

Sanchís and Martín Vázquez were the first to play for the first team of Real Madrid, making their debut at Murcia on December 4, 1983. Coach Alfredo Di Stéfano brought the youngsters in from the start. Both played surprisingly well and Sanchís even scored the winning goal. A few months later, February 5, 1984, saw the debut of Emilio Butragueño in an away game at Cádiz. *El Buitre* was an instant sensation and scored twice. Pardeza was added to the first team that same season and Míchel followed at the start of the next.

With La Quinta del Buitre (reduced to four members when Pardeza left the club for Zaragoza in 1986) Real Madrid had one of the best teams in Spain and Europe during the second half of the 1980s, winning amongst others two UEFA Cups and 5 Spanish championships in a row. Their record was only blemished by their failure to win the European Cup, and their continued abject defeats against the far superior AC Milan side of the time.

Martín Vázquez went to play for Torino in 1990. He made a return to Real Madrid in 1992, leaving the club again for good in 1995 (to Deportivo La Coruña). Butragueño left the club in 1995 and Michél in 1996. Both went to play for Atlético Celaya in Mexico.

Sanchís was the only member of La Quinta to never play for a club other than Real Madrid. By winning the Champions League twice (in 1998 and 2000), he also managed to accomplish what La Quinta had failed to achieve in its glory days. He retired in 2001 as last active member of the famous cohort at the age of 37.

The Lorenzo Sanz Era (1995-2000)

Casillas
Salgado
Karanka
Helguera
Campo
Carlos
McManaman
Redondo (C)
Raúl
Morientes
Anelka
2000 UEFA Champions League Final starting lineup.

After ten and a half years in office, Ramón Mendoza handed in his irrevocable resignation on 20 November 1995. He was relieved by Lorenzo Sanz, who held recourse to Club by-law 49 to get elected as heir to Mendoza by the 11 directors who continued in the Board of Directors following the transfer of power. On 20 May 1996, Lorenzo Sanz presented Fabio Capello as new head coach of Real Madrid. The Italian trainer landed in Madrid borne out by his five successful seasons with AC Milan, (with whom he won the 1994 European Cup) to replace Arsenio Iglesias who was the temp coach after the infamous Jorge Valdano quit. Although winining the league Capello left Madrid after just one season, years later he it was because he just didn't setaled in Madrid as well as he would have wanted, he came back to Milan. Replacing Fabio Capello was the German coach Jupp Heynckes led the team to win the very much awaited -last one was in 1966, 32 years earlier- European Cup. The venue: Amsterdam Arena. Date: 20 May 1998. The Merengues conquered their seventh top European trophy with a goal by Pedja Mijatovic against the Italian side of Juventus, who were the hot favourites that night. Heynckes was fired at the end of that year and been replaced by José Antonio Camacho who resegnated just monthes after on July, 2008 before the actual season even began.

Guus Hiddink was the manager in charge of guiding Real Madrid to their second Intercontinental Cup after the surprising resignation of Camacho. An extraordinary goal by Raúl in Tokyo sealed the more than fair 2-1 end result for the Whites. Hiddink was also fired just after less than a season, the Welshman John Toshack replaced him on February, 1999 he was fired 9 months later. making it 7 coaches in just 3 years.

Vicente del Bosque took over John Toshack as head coach of Real Madrid in mid-season and spearheaded the Madridistas towards raising their eighth European Cup -second Champions League title. The venue was superb: the newly built Saint-Denis stadium of Paris would host the first ever

Spanish final -as well as the first ever final of the European Cup between two teams of the same country- on 24 May 2000. It was a vibrant game which saw Madrid triumph over Valencia with a final 3-0 result. It was the last European Cup of the 20th Century and, as the first one, it belonged to the Whites.

The Florentino Pérez Era (2000-2006)

2000-2003: Dream Team

For more details on this topic, see Galáctico

César
Salgado
Hierro (C)
Helguera
Carlos
Makélélé
Figo
Solari
Zidane
Raúl
Morientes
2002 UEFA Champions League Final starting lineup.

In July 2000 Florentino Pérez was elected club president vowing to erase the club's debt and modernise the club's facilities, however the primary electoral promise that propelled Pérez to victory was the signing of then-FC Barcelona star Luís Figo. During the campaign, Pérez claimed he had an agreement with the Portuguese winger that would see Figo move to the Bernabeu should Pérez be elected. On July 16, Pérez won the election. Eight days later, Luís Figo was presented with the number 10 shirt of Real Madrid.

Days later, surrounded by controversy, Real Madrid idol Fernando Redondo, who had openly supported Pérez's opponent Lorenzo Sanz, was sold to Italian giants AC Milan. During the summer of 2000, Real Madrid signed Claude Makélélé, Albert Celades, Flávio Conceição, César Sánchez, Pedro Munitis, and Santiago Solari although aside from Makélélé and Conceição the rest had been signed prior to the election of Florentino Pérez. Expectations were high as Real Madrid began the 2000-01 season with the possibility of winning 5 trophies but stumbled at the first test losing the European Super Cup by a score of 1-2 to Galatasaray. An injury to Fernando Morientes left Real Madrid without a centre forward, but manager Vicente Del Bosque improvised by using youth team graduate Guti, in that role and Real Madrid made a good start to both domestic and European campaigns. But Real Madrid were defeated 2-0 at the Camp Nou against Barcelona and were later eliminated from the Copa del Rey by Toledo as well as losing the Intercontinental Cup final to a Boca Juniors side led by Martin Palermo and Riquelme. But Real Madrid recovered form and went top of the Spanish first division in mid-January, a position they would not relinquish on their way to winning the title. Real Madrid advanced from the second group stage of the Champions League to face Galatasaray in the quarterfinals. Real Madrid lost the first leg in Istanbul 3-2 but recovered to win the tie after a 3-0 victory in the Bernabeu. This would produce a replay of the 1999-2000 Champions League semifinal against Bayern Munich. Real Madrid would not reach the final however, losing 1-3 on aggregate to the eventual champions. Real Madrid would not be denied the league title however, and on 26 May, the merengues would crown themselves champions of the Spanish first division with an emphatic 5-0 win over Alaves at the Bernabeu. Goals by Raúl (2), Guti, Hierro, and Iván Helguera would ensure victory and Real Madrid's 28th league title with two matches left to play.

After reaching an agreement to re-zone and sell the Ciudad Deportiva, Pérez went on to sign Zinédine Zidane (2001), Ronaldo (2002) and David Beckham (2003). The media began referring to the team as Los Galácticos. Initially the strategy, eventually dubbed Zidanes y Pavones and meant to combine world stars and youth team graduates, was successful and Real Madrid won La Liga in 2001 and 2003 and the UEFA Champions League in 2002, their centenary year. They also won the Intercontinental Cup, the European Super Cup and the Supercopa de España in both 2001 and 2003.

Off the field the Zidanes y Pavones policy resulted in increased financial success based on the exploitation of the club's high marketing potential around the world, especially in Asia.

In the summer of 2003, just after capturing another La Liga title, Florentino Pérez and the board of directors refused to renew the contract of coach Vicente Del Bosque and after an internal dispute forced captain Fernando Hierro to leave the club. They also ignored Claude Makélélé's request of a new contract with a better salary, in return, Makélélé asked for a transfer request, and was transferred to Chelsea.

2003/2004 Season: Wind of Change

The few days after the capturing of the league title were surrounded with controversy. The first controversial decision came when Perez sacked winning coach Vicente del Bosque, after Real's sporting director claimed that del Bosque was not the right man for the job; they wanted someone young to shake up the team. The bad atmosphere continued when the Real legend and captain Fernando Hierro left the club after a disagreement with the management, as did Steve McManaman. However, the club toured Asia in preseason and introduced newly signed galactico David Beckham. Perez and his directors refused to renew Claude Makélélé's contract with a better salary, upsetting Makelele who asked for a transfer, eventually moving to Chelsea FC. In the final days of the transfer window, Fernando Morientes left the club on loan to Monaco. Real Madrid, with newly appointed coach Carlos

Queiroz, started their domestic league slowly after a hard win over Real Betis.

But everyone was convinced when Madrid won 7-2 at home over Real Valladolid. The second part of the season gave chances to youngsters and academy graduates like Borja Fernandez, Alvaro Mejia, Antonio Nunez, and Juanfran to shine, as Queiroz rotated his squad, although the team missed Portillo whose previous poor performances inspired the club to loan him in the winter to the Italian side ACF Fiorentina. Real Madrid also topped their group in the Champions League and advanced to the quarter-finals after defeating Bayern Munich in the Last-16 2-1 on aggregate. But Madrid's on-loan striker Morientes punished his team with his goals, as Madrid saw Monaco go on to the semis. However Real kept their morale high after leading La Liga, 8 points clear of Valencia CF in February. But some surprises were waiting them, as they were beaten for the first time at the Bernabeu that season at the hands of CA Osasuna 3-0. They recovered their points lead after a win at the Vicente Calderón Stadium, but more disappointments were to come as they lost their final 5 games in the league at home to RCD Mallorca, Arch rivals FC Barcelona, Real Sociedad, and away to Real Murcia and Deportivo de La Coruña. They saw teams like Valencia, Barcelona, and Deportivo pass them to make up the top three, as Real ended the season in a disappointing 4th place. Their poor performances continued as they lost the final of the Copa Del Rey to Real Zaragoza. Shortly after the end of the season, Carlos Queiroz was sacked and replaced by ex-Real Madrid player, José Antonio Camacho.

2004/05 Season

Perez appointed club legend Jose Antonio Camacho as head coach after Queiroz was sacked. Camacho highlighted the team's bad defensive performances and persuaded Perez to spend a total of €45 millions on Argentine defender Walter Samuel and English centre back Jonathan Woodgate but missed out on signing Arsenal's midfield general, Patrick Vieira due to Vieira's boldness of asking for a 'Galactico' paycheck (like Figo, Zidane, Ronaldo and David Beckham but unlike Claude Makélélé, who left for exactly that reason - €6 million Euros per year). The summer of 2004 also saw the sale of Cameroon Striker Samuel Eto'o, who had been loaned out to Real Mallorca, to arch rivals F.C. Barcelona.

English striker Michael Owen was bought from Liverpool F.C. but never settled at Real Madrid while Eto'o went on to great success with Barcelona. Camacho resigned as head coach because of the bad performances and was replaced by Mariano García Remón. García Remón's last game was a loss at the hand of Sevilla FC, where the eventual champions F.C. Barcelona were 6 points clear from their nearest rivals, and Madrid sat in 5th position. Remón was replaced by Luxemburgo after the winter break, who then signed Thomas Gravesen from Everton to fill the hole in midfield. Madrid failed to progress to the Quarter-finals of the Champions League as in the Copa Del Rey, but under Luxemburgo Madrid fought hard to earn second place with 80 points, 4 points behind Barcelona.

2005/06 season: End of an Era

The 2005-06 season began with the promise of several new signings — Julio Baptista (€20 Million), Robinho (€30 Million) and Sergio Ramos (€30 Million - Release Clause) —, but the Brazilian coach was not able to find the right formula on the pitch as Real Madrid's poor form continued, with the team hitting rock bottom after a humiliating 0-3 loss at the hands of F.C. Barcelona in the Santiago Bernabeu. Luxemburgo would eventually resign and his replacement was Juan Ramón López Caro, formally the manager of Real Madrid Castilla. A brief return to form came to an abrupt halt after losing the first leg of the Copa del Rey quarterfinal, 6-1 to Real Zaragoza. Shortly after, Real Madrid were eliminated from the Champions League for a fourth successive year, this time at the hands of Arsenal. On February 27, 2006, Florentino Pérez resigned. Real Madrid eventually managed to finish second in the league but did not pose a serious threat to defending champions, F.C. Barcelona.

The Ramón Calderón Era (2006-2009)

On July 2, 2006 Ramón Calderón was elected as club president and subsequently appointed Fabio Capello as the new coach and Predrag Mijatović as the new sporting director. As new manager of Real Madrid, Capello signed the World Cup winning captain Fabio Cannavaro and Emerson, both from embattled Juventus, for a total sum of €23 m; Ruud van Nistelrooy from Manchester United for €15 m; Mahamadou Diarra from Lyon for €26 m and on a last minute trade loan - José Antonio Reyes, with Julio Baptista going the other way, after a disappointing time at Madrid. Ramon failed, however, to sign A.C. Milan star Kaká, Arsenal star Cesc Fàbregas and Chelsea star Arjen Robben as was promised by the new president. During the January transfer window, he has managed to sign Fluminense left back Marcelo (€6.5 m), River Plate forward Gonzalo Higuaín (€13 m) and Boca Juniors midfielder Fernando Gago (€18 m).

2006–07 season

On 16 January 2007, Calderón made some very unfortunate comments about the behavior of some players in the squad and the Santiago Bernabéu fans, which has put the club in a delicate situation. One of the players that Calderón criticised was David Beckham, who, in January 2007, agreed to a deal to play for the Los Angeles Galaxy at the end of that season. Among others to criticise Beckham was manager Fabio Capello, who at the time vowed never to select Beckham for the team again, although he later withdrew his words. At the end of January, Ronaldo left the club for €7.5 million for Milan. On 9 February 2007, Capello allowed Beckham back onto Real's starting 11 in an away match against Real Sociedad. Beckham played well and scored the equalizing goal in the match (Real Madrid won the match 2–1). On 24 February 2007, the Madrid derby between Atlético Madrid and Real Madrid at the Vicente Calderón Stadium was a 1–1 draw. The scorers were Fernando Torres for Atlético, and Gonzalo Higuaín for Real. The Madrid derby is seen as one of the most fiercely contested matches in the Spanish football calendar.

On 7 March 2007 Real Madrid failed to reach the quarter-finals of the Champions League due to Bayern Munich's strong home performance. Despite winning the home leg 3–2, they lost 2–1 in Germany and were eliminated on an away goals tiebreaker. Bayern scored the fastest goal in the Champions league during that match, after Roberto Carlos lost the ball after kick-off, which led to Roy Makaay scoring in 10 seconds.

On 10 March 2007, Real Madrid contested the Clasico against Barcelona at the Camp Nou. Real Madrid took the lead three times after two goals from Ruud van Nistelrooy and one from Sergio Ramos but were pegged back by a hat-trick from Lionel Messi, including an injury-time equaliser. Despite the sending off of Oleguer, the Clasico ended 3–3.

Real Madrid managed to find their form consistently for the first time all season as they managed to win seven out of eight of the final twelve games, including a 2–1 home win over Valencia on 21 April 2007 and another 3–2 home win over Sevilla on 6 May 2007. Calderón then went on to say that if the team keep up their great play, he was confident Real Madrid will win the league title and end their four year wait for a major trophy on June 17.

On 12 May 2007, despite not having Robinho and Beckham on the pitch (due to separate yellow cards given in the previous match against Sevilla) Real Madrid took over first place in the La Liga for the first time all season by defeating Espanyol 4–3, coming back from 1–3 first half deficit. Los Blancos were able to avoid a 3-3 draw thanks to a 89th minute goal by Gonzalo Higuaín.

The Sunday after Real won their epic battle with Espanyol, Barça dropped points with a 1–1 draw to struggling Betis. By virtue of their superior head to head record, Real Madrid sat at the top of La Liga, with four crucial games left to play.

The following Sunday, Real managed to beat Recreativo de Huelva 2–3 at the Nuevo Colombino. With the score tied at 2–2, Real Madrid looked set return the lead back to rivals Barcelona until Roberto Carlos scored at the end of the match from a Fernando Gago assist and the squad left Huelva with just three games left to play. The remaining three were Deportivo de La Coruña, Real Zaragoza and Mallorca.

On May 26, 2007, Real Madrid did another excellent match to defeat Deportivo 3-1 at the Bernabéu. This victory made it six wins in a row for Real Madrid. Goals from Sergio Ramos, Raúl and Ruud van Nistelrooy secured the win. That victory left Real with only two games left to play and with hopes and morale reaching a high point in Real's dressing room, Capello and Calderón began to believe that Real was going to win the league title.

On June 9, 2007, Real played against Zaragoza at La Romareda. The match got off to a bad start when Real Madrid were forced to change their lineup some minutes before the start of the match when young defender Miguel Torres got injured in the warm up, tearing his hamstring. Zaragoza led Real 2-1 near the end of the match while Barcelona were also winning against Espanyol 2-1. Real's title challenge looked to be over. However, a late Ruud Van Nistelrooy equalizer followed by a last minute Raúl Tamudo goal sprang Real Madrid's title hopes back into their favor. Sevilla were also held 0-0 away against Mallorca, which meant that a win at home against Mallorca would effectively secure Los Merengues their 30th Spanish league title.

The title was won on 17 June, Real faced Mallorca at the Bernabéu, while Barcelona and Sevilla, the other title challengers, faced Gimnàstic de Tarragona and Villarreal respectively. At half time Real were 0-1 down, while Barcelona had surged ahead into a 0-3 lead in Tarragona; however, three goals in the last half-an-hour secured Real Madrid a 3-1 win and their first league title since 2003. The first goal came from Reyes who scored after a good work from Higuaín. An own goal followed by another delightful goal from Reyes allowed Real to begin celebrating the title. Thousands of Real Madrid fans began going to Plaza de Cibeles to celebrate the title.

Real Madrid recently signed a three-year deal with betting company Bwin.com in June, announcing a shirt deal at the same time that saw Benq Siemens replaced by Bwin.com on the front. The 2007-08 shirts made their first appearance during their title celebration on June 17, 2007.

2007–09 season

On 25 August, Real Madrid kicked off the season in a derby against city rivals Atlético Madrid at the Santiago Bernabéu. It was a highly entertaining display from both sides but Real managed to win 2–1, with goals from Raúl and Wesley Sneijder for Real while Sergio Agüero scored for Atlético. It was a great start for Real as they showed skill and that they were adapting to the new style of play Bernd Schuster had brought in. On 28 August, Antonio Puerta, player of Sevilla, died after three days in the hospital. The Santiago Bernabéu Trophy – where Real Madrid was about to play against Sporting Clube de Portugal – was cancelled in honor of Puerta. On 2 September, Real Madrid managed to win 5–0 against Villarreal at the El Madrigal, with two goals from Sneijder, one from Raúl, one from Ruud van Nistelrooy, and one from Guti. Real extended their winning streak to three after they beat Almería at home before earning a well deserved 1–1 against Real Valladolid, with Javier Saviola scoring the equalizer three minutes from final time.

Four days later, Real remained unbeaten as they beat Real Betis 2–0 at the Bernabéu, with goals from Raúl and an amazing bicycle kick from Júlio Baptista. Real continued their unbeaten run under Schuster by beating Getafe 1–0 away to ensure *Los Blancos* remain at the summit of the La Liga.

Real Madrid has closed out its best fiscal year in history after recording €351 million in ordinary revenue – a 20% increase compared to last year – and €83 million in earnings before interest, taxes, depreciation, and amortization – a 43% increase compared to the 2005–06 fiscal year.

Real started their European Campaign well, beating German side Werder Bremen 2–1 at home thanks to goals from Raúl and van Nistelrooy. However, they lost in the first knockout round against Roma, with a score of 4–2.

On 9 December, it was announced that Bernd Schuster had been sacked as manager, and that ex-Tottenham Hotspur manager Juande Ramos would replace him.

However Real Madrid once again went out of the Champions League at the last 16 stage, for the fourth time in a row, with a humiliating 5-0 aggregate defeat against Liverpool.

The second Florentino Pérez Era (2009–*present*)

After no one of the 2009 presidency election was able to get the necessary funds (€56 million), on 1 June, Florentino Pérez was officially announced as Real Madrid president. His first move as Real Madrid president was to sign Brazilian superstar Kaká from Milan for an undisclosed fee believed to be £56 million or €68 million. On 11 June 2009, Real Madrid officially announced on their website that an £80 million or €94 million offer for Portuguese Ballon d'Or winner Cristiano Ronaldo had been accepted by his club, Manchester United, after the player had expressed his desire to leave the club for *Los Merengues*.

On 25 June 2009, Raúl Albiol joined Real Madrid on a fee thought to be in the region of €15 million.

On 26 June 2009, the deal for Cristiano Ronaldo was finalized with the player becoming officially a Real Madrid player on 1 July 2009.

On 1 July 2009, it was announced that Olympique Lyonnais had reached an agreement with Spanish club Real Madrid for the transfer of Karim Benzema. The transfer fee was priced at €35 million with the fee rising to as much as €41 million based on incentives.

On 29 July 2009, it was announced that Real Madrid and Liverpool had reached an agreement on the transfer of Alvaro Arbeloa to the Spanish club. A fee of €4 million the same amount Liverpool F.C paid for the player in January 2007 had been agreed between the clubs and the player would sign a five-year contract with Real Madrid.

On 5 August 2009, Xabi Alonso was announced as Real Madrid's latest signing with Liverpool receiving around £30 million for the transfer of the Spanish midfielder.

Real Madrid opened the 2009–10 season with a 3–2 home win over Deportivo La Coruña, with the goals scored by Raúl, Cristiano Ronaldo, and Lassana Diarra. On 15 September 2009, Real Madrid achieved their first Champions League win in the Group Stage against Zürich, winning 5–2 in Zürich. On 4 October 2009, after seven consecutive wins in all the competitions, Real Madrid lost for the first time of the season, in the Ramón Sánchez Pizjuán, 2–1 to Sevilla. On 27 October 2009, Real Madrid were defeated 4-0 by third tier team Alcorcón in the round of 32 first leg of the King's Cup.

Grounds

Santiago Bernabéu Stadium

El Bernabéu	

Full name	Estadio Santiago Bernabeu
Former names	Nuevo Estadio Chamartín (1947–1955)
Location	Madrid, Spain
Coordinates	40°27′10″N 3°41′17″W
Broke ground	27 October 1944
Built	1944-1947
Opened	14 December 1947
Renovated	1982, 2001
Expanded	1953, 1992, 1994
Owner	Real Madrid C.F.
Operator	Real Madrid C.F.
Surface	Desso GrassMaster
Construction cost	288,342,653.72 €
Architect	Manuel Muñoz Monasterio Luis Alemany Soler Antonio Lamela (Expansion)
Capacity	80,354
Field dimensions	107 × 72 m (351 × 236 ft)

Tenants
Real Madrid C.F. Spain National Football Team

The **Estadio Santiago Bernabéu** (Spanish pronunciation: [esˈtaðjo sanˈtjaɣo βernaˈβeu]) is an all-seater football stadium in Madrid, Spain. It was inaugurated on 14 December 1947 and is owned by Real Madrid C.F. It has a current capacity of 80,354 spectators.

El Bernabéu, re-named in honour of their former chairman Santiago Bernabéu Yeste, is one of the world's most famous and prestigious football venues.[*citation needed*] It has hosted the European Cup final on three occasions: in 1957, 1969 and 1980, and the UEFA Champions League Final in 2010. The finals for the 1964 European Nations' Cup and the 1982 World Cup have also been held at the Bernabéu.

Location

The Santiago Bernabéu is located on the Paseo de la Castellana, in the district of Chamartín. It occupies the block bounded by the *Paseo de la Castellana* and the streets of *Concha Espina*, *Padre Damián*, and *Rafael Salgado*.

History

On 22 June 1944, the *Banco Mercantil e Industrial* bank granted a credit to Santiago Bernabéu and Rafael Salgado for the purchase of the land adjacent to the old Chamartín Stadium. On 5 September 1944, architects Manuel Muñoz Monasterio and Luis Alemany Soler were hired and the structure on the site began to give way to the new stadium. On 27 October 1944, construction work on the stadium began.

The *Nuevo Estadio Chamartín* (English: *New Chamartín Stadium*) was inaugurated on 14 December 1947 with a match between Real Madrid FC and the Portuguese side Os Belenenses. The stadium had an initial capacity of 75,145 spectators, 27,645 of which had seats (7,125 covered) and 47,500 for standing fans. Sabino Barinaga was the first player to score in the new stadium.

The 1950s

The first major renovation occurred in 1954. On June 19 of that year the stadium expanded to accommodate 125,000 spectators. Thus, the Madrid coliseum became the biggest stadium of all the participants of the newly established European Cup.

On 4 January 1955, after the General Assembly of Members Compromisaros, it was decided that the stadium adopt its present name in honour of the club president Santiago Bernabéu.

In May 1957, Real Madrid used electric stadium lighting in a game against Sport Recife of Brazil.

The 1980s

The next big changes did not occur until the early 1980s with the hosting of the 1982 FIFA World Cup in Spain. The stadium had to adapt to the changing times and with this, architects Rafael Luis Alemany and Manuel Salinas were hired for the stadium's renovation project. The brothers were sons of Luis Alemany Alemany Soler, who carried out the original construction project next to Munoz Monasterio. The work lasted 16 months and had a cost of 704 million pesetas, of which 530 million was paid by the city of Madrid.

The improvements included a number of points. First, FIFA forced two-thirds of the seating area to be covered. For this reason, Real Madrid installed a roof covering the perimeter of the first and second tiers of seating, except the east side. Thus, the stadium's capacity was reduced from 120,000 to 90,800 spectators, 24,550 of which were covered by the new roof. The project also involved remodelling the façade, the installation of new electronic signs in the north and south ends, as well as the renovation of the press areas, lockers rooms, access, and ancillary areas.

The stadium hosted four matches in the World Cup: three second-round Group 2 matches (West Germany vs. England, West Germany vs. Spain, and Spain vs. England) and the final between Italy and West Germany.

The 1990s

In the mid 1980s, UEFA introduced new safety standards due to increased violence in the stadiums of Europe. Therefore, The stadium was forced to create separate shortcuts to different stadium sections and seats for all spectators. In the 1990s the Santiago Bernabéu went through a large expansion and remodeling. The board of Ramón Mendoza awarded the project to *Gines Navarro Construcciones, S.A.*

The work started on 7 February 1992 and concluded on 7 May 1994 with a final cost of more than pts 5 billion, substantially raising the debt of the club, having no institutional support.

The work concluded with the creation of an amphitheater on the west side and in the foundations, coupled with the existing building by using hydraulic jacks.

In total, 20,200 upgraded seats were installed, with each seat having a tilt of 87 degrees, ensuring a perfect view and proximity to the pitch. In addition, to access the new ring, four entrance towers were erected on the outside, each with two staircases and a central spiral ramp.

With the new structure, the height of the stadium was increased from 22 m to 45 m. This caused problems during the winter, leaving two-thirds of the field of play in the shade. This lack of sunlight led to grass deterioration on the pitch. For this reason, a polypropylene pipe network was installed at a 20 cm depth under the pitch. At over 30 km long the pipe system circulates hot water, keeping the turf from freezing in cold temperatures.

Also, due to the height of the stand, it was necessary to improve and increase the lighting capability. A retractable protective roof was also installed to protect the fans from the elements. After the renovation, the stadium's capacity was 110,000 spectators.

Already in the summer of 1998, and chaired by Lorenzo Sanz, the Santiago Bernabéu adopted an all-seating arrangement, bringing its capacity down to 75,328 spectators.

The 2000s

Real Madrid at the Santiago Bernabéu in 2007

When Florentino Pérez became the president of Real Madrid, he launched a "master plan" with one goal: to improve the comfort of the Santiago Bernabéu and the quality of its facilities, and maximise revenue for the stadium.

Pérez invested €127 million in five years (2001–2006) by adding an expansion to the east side of the stadium, as well adding a new façade on Father Damien street, new costumes, new boxes and VIP areas, a new stage in honour of the east side, a new press area (also located on the east side), a new audio system, new bars, integration of heating in the stands, panoramic lifts, new restaurants, escalators in the tower access, and implementation of the multipurpose building in Father Damien street.

Following the enlargement of the lateral east side and the creation of new galleries, the capacity of the Santiago Bernabéu is 80,354, all seated.

In 2007, the 1,000th game was played at the Santiago Bernabéu. In addition, the latest revision of UEFA on 27 October 2007, on the occasion of Champions League match against Olympiacos, served as a final step to give the Santiago Bernabéu elite stadium status on 14 November 2007, a month before the celebration of the 60th anniversary of the inauguration of the stadium. UEFA announced that the club will officially rename the Elite stadium.

Pérez proposed construction of a retractable roof before he resigned in 2005. In 2009, following the re-election of Pérez as the club president, it was announced that the roof construction was looking unlikely due to the financial situation of the club. However, according to Spanish sports newspaper

Marca, Pérez wants to restructure Santiago Bernabéu. According to the newspaper, the architect in charge will be chosen from among a shortlist of Spanish architects Santiago Calatrava and Pritzker Prize-winner Rafael Moneo, and Chinese-American Ieoh Ming Pei, also a Pritzker winner.

The stadium was officially announced the venue for the 2010 UEFA Champions League Final in a star-studded ceremony in Nyon in 2008. However, Real Madrid was eliminated in the Round of 16 of the 2009-10 Champions League, while FC Barcelona had advanced to the semi-finals. Barça fans became obsessed with reaching the final and winning the tournament in their arch-rival's home ground, being seen as the ultimate humiliation to Madrid, leading to several Madrid newspapers criticizing former Real Madrid president Ramon Calderon for the successful bid to host the final. When Barcelona was eliminated by Internazionale on April 28, 2010, Madrid fans and the media celebrated. In the final on 22 May 2010, Internazionale defeated Bayern Munich by 2–0.

Transportation

The stadium is served by its own metro station along the Line 10 called *Santiago Bernabéu*. It is also served by the following bus routes: 14, 27, 40, 43, 120, 147 and 150.

External links

- Media related to Santiago Bernabéu Stadium at Wikimedia Commons
- Santiago Bernabéu Stadium at Google Maps [1]
- Santiago Bernabéu Stadium Facts and Photos [2]
- Santiago Bernabéu Stadium [3]
- Santiago Bernabéu Stadium Description and Photos [4] (Spanish)
- Virtual Stadium Tour [5]
- Real Madrid Football Club Official website [6]
- Real Madrid Football Club Fan site [7]
- 360 Degree Image of the Stadium [8]

This template requires you to use a title as the title parameter one of the succesion box headers as it's header parameter.

Alfredo di Stéfano Stadium

Full name	Estadio Alfredo di Stéfano
Location	Valdebebas, Madrid, Spain
Coordinates	40°28′37″N 3°36′51″W
Built	2006
Opened	9 May 2006
Owner	Real Madrid
Surface	Grass
Architect	Antonio Lamela
Capacity	6,000 24,000 (On completion of expansion)
Field dimensions	105 x 68 m
Tenants	
Real Madrid Castilla	

Alfredo di Stéfano Stadium is a multi-purpose stadium in Madrid, Spain. It is currently used for football matches and is the home ground of Real Madrid Castilla, the reserve team of Real Madrid. The stadium holds 6,000 people. It is named after former Real footballer Alfredo di Stéfano.

The venue is part of the Ciudad Real Madrid, the club's new training facilities located outside Madrid in Valdebebas. On Tuesday 9 May 2006 the Alfredo di Stéfano Stadium was inaugurated at the City of Madrid where Real Madrid usually trains. The inaugural match was between Real Madrid and Stade de Reims, a rematch of the European Cup final won by Real Madrid in 1956. Real Madrid won the inaugural match 6-1 with goals from Sergio Ramos, Antonio Cassano (2), Roberto Soldado (2), and José Manuel Jurado.

References

Geographical coordinates: 40°28′36″N 3°36′51″W

Estadio Chamartín

Full name	Estadio Chamartín
Location	Madrid, Spain
Opened	17 May 1923
Closed	1947
Owner	Real Madrid
Operator	Real Madrid
Architect	José María Castell
Capacity	22,500
Tenants	
Real Madrid	

Estadio Chamartín was a multi-use stadium in Madrid, Spain. It was initially used as the stadium of Real Madrid matches before Santiago Bernabéu Stadium opened in 1947. The stadium held 22,500 people and was built in 1923. The first match at the stadium was Real Madrid against Newcastle United. It is featured in the EA Sports video game FIFA 10

Rivalries

El Clásico

The respective captains of Madrid and Barcelona, Casillas and Puyol.	
City or region	Barcelona and Madrid (Spain)
First contested	17 February 1902
Teams involved	FC Barcelona, Real Madrid
Most wins	Real Madrid (68)
Most recent meeting	0–2 (Real Madrid – Barcelona)
Next meeting	28 November 2010 (Barcelona – Real Madrid)
Largest victory	11-1 Real Madrid - Barcelona (year 1943)

El Clásico (English: *The Classic*), also known as *El derbi Español* or *El Clàssic* is the name generically given to any football match between Real Madrid and FC Barcelona. It is contested at least bi-annually as part of the Spanish La Liga competition, with a maximum of six matches a year, with two extra in Copa del Rey and Champions League respectively. Other than the UEFA Champions League Final, it is the most followed club football match in the world, watched by hundreds of millions of people.

The rivalry comes about as Madrid and Barcelona are the two largest cities in Spain, and the two clubs are the most successful and influential football clubs in the country. Real Madrid has amassed 73 trophies and Barcelona 68, while Athletic Bilbao comes third with 32 trophies. They are sometimes identified with opposing political positions, with Real Madrid and Barcelona representing Spanish nationalism and Catalan nationalism respectively.

Rivalry

The Primo de Rivera and Franco years

As early as the 1930s, Barcelona "had developed a reputation as a symbol of Catalan pride and identity, opposed to the centralising tendencies of Madrid". During the Franco dictatorship, most citizens of Barcelona were in strong opposition to the fascist-like régime, with several players of Barcelona enrolling with the opposition forces in 1934 Wikipedia:Please clarify. . On a representative level, the president of Barcelona Josep Sunyol was killed by Franco's security police as part of his political activities while visited Republican troops north of Madrid. Phil Ball, the author of *Morbo: The Story of Spanish Football*, calls the El Clásico "a re-enactment of the Spanish Civil War".

Though the first socialist party in Spain was founded in Madrid, almost all the ideas that have shaped the country's modern history – republicanism, federalism, anarchism, syndicalism and communism – have been introduced via the region of Catalonia, where Barcelona is. During the dictatorships of Miguel Primo de Rivera and of Francisco Franco, all regional languages and identities were frowned upon and restrained. In this period FC Barcelona gained their motto *més que un club* (*English: More than a club*) because of its alleged connection to progressive beliefs and its representative role for Catalonia. However, during Franco's regime, the blaugrana team seemed to be granted profit due to its good relationship with the dictator at management level. In any case, for most of the Catalans, and many other Spaniards as well, Real Madrid was regarded as the establishment club, in spite of the fact that during the Spanish Civil War, presidents of both clubs like Josep Sunyol and Rafael Sánchez Guerra, suffered in the Spanish Civil War.

Di Stéfano transfer

The rivalry was intensified during the 1950s when the clubs disputed the signing of Alfredo di Stéfano. Di Stéfano had impressed both Barcelona and Real Madrid whilst playing for Club Deportivo Los Millonarios in Bogota, during a players' strike in his native Argentina. Both Madrid and Barcelona attempted to sign him and, due to confusion that emerged from di Stéfano moving to Millonarios from River Plate following the strike, both clubs claimed to own his registration. After intervention from FIFA representative Muñoz Calero it was decided that both Barcelona and Real Madrid had to share the player in alternate seasons. Barcelona's Franco-imposed President backed down after a few appearances as Barcelona's side claimed but Real say Barcelona's decision was voluntary, and di Stefano moved definitively to Madrid.

Di Stéfano became integral in the subsequent success achieved by Madrid, scoring twice in his first game against Barcelona. With him, Madrid won the initial five European Champions Cup competitions. The 1960s saw the rivalry reach the European stage when they met twice at the European Cup, Real Madrid winning in 1960 and FC Barcelona winning in 1961.

Current issues

When Luis Figo returned to Barcelona as a Real Madrid player, the Barcelona support group Boixos Nois threw a pig's head after him.

The two teams met again in the UEFA Champions League semi-final in 2002. The match, dubbed by Spanish media as the *Match of the Century*, was watched by more than 500 million people. In the Clásico held on November 2005, Barcelona played away in Madrid. The star of the Barcelona team was Ronaldinho, who became the first Barcelona player to receive a standing ovation from Real Madrid fans.

The rivalry has been strengthened throughout time by the internal transfer of players between the clubs. Barcelona players who have later played for Real Madrid include Bernd Schuster, who switched in 1988, Michael Laudrup went to Real Madrid on a free transfer in 1994, but the most notorious was former vice-captain Luís Figo's switch in 2000. Players transferring from Real Madrid to Barcelona are less frequent, the most recent being Luis Enrique, who went to Barcelona in 1996 where he went on to captain the Blaugrana, and since 2008 coach the reserve team.

A 2007 survey by the *Centro de Investigaciones Sociológicas* determined that Real Madrid was the team with the largest following in Spain. Thirty-two percent of the Spanish population supported Real Madrid, while 25 percent supported Barcelona. In third place came Valencia CF, who were supported by five percent. Barcelona in turn is more popular in Europe than Madrid. According to a survey made by the German research agency Sport+Markt in 2010, Barcelona has approximately 57,8 million fans around Europe, while Real Madrid has 31,3 million fans. Globally, Real Madrid is the most popular football club in the world according to a study performed by Harvard University in 2007, with over 228 million supporters worldwide.

League matches

These are only the league matches, club name in **bold** indicate win. The score is given at half-time (T) and full-time (H), in the goals columns the goalscorer and time when goal was scored is noted.

Game	Date	Round	Home team	Away team	Score (H/T)	Goals (home)	Goals (away)
1	17 February 1929	2	FC Barcelona	**Real Madrid**	**1–2** (0–1)	Parera (70)	Morera (10, 55)
2	9 May 1929	11	Real Madrid	**FC Barcelona**	**0–1** (0–0)		Sastre (83)
3	26 January 1930	9	FC Barcelona	**Real Madrid**	**1–4** (0–3)	Bestit (63)	Rubio (10, 37), F. López (17), Lazcano (71)
4	30 March 1930	18	**Real Madrid**	FC Barcelona	**5–1** (3–0)	Rubio (5, 23), Lazcano (42, 68, 72)	Goiburu (84)
5	1 February 1931	9	Real Madrid	FC Barcelona	**0–0** (0–0)		
6	5 April 1931	18	**FC Barcelona**	Real Madrid	**3–1** (2–1)	Ramón (12, 35, 73)	Eugenio (38)
7	31 January 1932	9	**Real Madrid**	FC Barcelona	**2–0** (2–0)	Olivares (26, 40)	
8	3 April 1932	18	FC Barcelona	Real Madrid	**2–2** (1–1)	Samitier (20), Arocha (p. 87)	Lazcano (43), Regueiro (70)
9	1 January 1933	6	FC Barcelona	Real Madrid	**1–1** (0–0)	Arocha (68)	Regueiro (p. 78)
10	5 March 1933	15	**Real Madrid**	FC Barcelona	**2–1** (1–0)	Samitier (35, 68)	Goiburu (89)
11	26 November 1933	4	FC Barcelona	**Real Madrid**	**1–2** (0–2)	Morera (46)	Olivares (9), Regueiro (26)
12	28 January 1934	13	**Real Madrid**	FC Barcelona	**4–0** (3–0)	Valle (7), Samitier (20), Regueiro (30), Eugenio (50)	
13	3 February 1935	10	**Real Madrid**	FC Barcelona	**8–2** (5–1)	Lazcano (14, 42, 73), Sañudo (21, 35, 47, 81), Regueiro (29)	Escola (17), Guzmán (68)
14	21 April 1935	81	**FC Barcelona**	Real Madrid	**5–0** (1–0)	Ventolrà (43, 62, 68, 82), Escola (48)	
15	26 December 1935	7	FC Barcelona	**Real Madrid**	**0–3** (0–2)		Regueiro (21), Diz (40), Lecue (47)

16	22 March 1936	18	**Real Madrid**	FC Barcelona	**3–0** (2–0)	Lecue (10, 47), Emilin (43)	
17	28 January 1940	9	**Real Madrid**	FC Barcelona	**2–1** (1–1)	Alonso (1'), Lecue (75')	Pascual (3')
18	14 April 1940	20	FC Barcelona	Real Madrid	**0–0** (0–0)		
19	1 December 1940	10	**FC Barcelona**	Real Madrid	**3–0** (0–0)	Sospedra (49, 69), Valle Mas (53)	
20	23 February 1941	21	Real Madrid	**FC Barcelona**	**1–2** (0–0)	Barinaga (49)	Bravo (60), Martín (63)
21	19 October 1941	4	**Real Madrid**	FC Barcelona	**4–3** (2–1)	Arbiza (17, 70), Benito (o.g. 35), Belmar (55)	Calvet (25), Raich (60), Gracia (87)
22	25 January 1942	17	FC Barcelona	**Real Madrid**	**0–2** (0–0)		Alday (63, 78)
23	27 September 1942	1	**Real Madrid**	FC Barcelona	**3–0** (1–0)	Arbiza (7, 89), Alsúa (52)	
24	10 January 1943	14	FC Barcelona	Real Madrid	**5–5** (4–1)	Martín (25, 40), Escola (31), Valle Mas (32, 62)	Alonso (10), Alday (27, 51), Botella (74), Mardones II (87)
25	2 January 1944	13	Real Madrid	**FC Barcelona**	**0–1** (0–0)		Valle Mas (50)
26	9 April 1944	26	FC Barcelona	**Real Madrid**	**1–2** (1–0)	Escola (31)	Alsúa (62), Rosalénch (o.g. 71)
27	9 November 1944	8	**Real Madrid**	FC Barcelona	**1–0** (1–0)	Moleiro (21)	
28	25 March 1945	21	**FC Barcelona**	Real Madrid	**5–0** (1–0)	César (41, 46), Bravo (52), Escola (77), Gonzalvo III (86)	
29	25 November 1945	9	**Real Madrid**	FC Barcelona	**3–2** (1–0)	Barinaga (23), Pruden (61), Belmar (68)	Martín (51), Gonzalvo III (75)
30	3 March 1946	22	**FC Barcelona**	Real Madrid	**1–0** (1–0)	César (17)	
31	1 December 1946	11	**Real Madrid**	FC Barcelona	**2–1** (1–1)	Corona (p. 4), Molowny (79)	Seguer (23)
32	30 March 1947	24	**FC Barcelona**	Real Madrid	**3–2** (2–0)	Bravo (18), Navarro (39, 49)	Arsuaga (48, 60)
33	12 October 1947	4	Real Madrid	FC Barcelona	**1–1** (0–1)	Barinaga (65)	Clemente (o.g. 31)

34	25 January 1948	17	**FC Barcelona**	Real Madrid	**4–2** (3–0)	Seguer (2), Basora (28, 58), César (43)	Gallardo (68), Rafa Yunta (76)
35	19 September 1948	2	Real Madrid	**FC Barcelona**	**1–2** (0–1)	Barinaga (60)	Caffaratti (41), Basora (48)
36	15 January 1949	16	**FC Barcelona**	Real Madrid	**3–1** (1–1)	César (28, 61), Basora (56)	Pahiño (9)
37	18 September 1949	3	**Real Madrid**	FC Barcelona	**6–1** (3–0)	Olmedo (2), Cabrera (4), Pahiño (40, 68), Macala (62, 69)	Gonzalvo II (85)
38	15 January 1950	16	FC Barcelona	**Real Madrid**	**2–3** (1–0)	Basora (41), César (53)	Pahiño (58), Rafa Verdu (66), Cabrera (73)
39	24 September 1950	3	**FC Barcelona**	Real Madrid	**7–2** (3–1)	Nicolau (9, 56), César (14), Marcos Aureli (39, 88), Gonzalvo III (62), Basora (82)	Molowny (15), García González (66)
40	14 January 1951	18	**Real Madrid**	FC Barcelona	**4–1** (4–1)	Narro (8, 17, 29), Pahiño (13)	Canal (31)
41	11 November 1951	10	**Real Madrid**	FC Barcelona	**5–1** (3–1)	Molowny (3), Cabrera (32), Pahiño (35, 87), Roque Olsen (57)	Basora (44)
42	2 March 1952	25	**FC Barcelona**	Real Madrid	**4–2** (2–2)	Vila Soler (13), César (36, 56, 74)	Roque Olsen (33), Arsuaga (39)
43	23 November 1952	11	**Real Madrid**	FC Barcelona	**2–1** (0–0)	Arsuaga (76, 80)	Manchón (67)
44	5 April 1953	26	**FC Barcelona**	Real Madrid	**1–0** (1–0)	Moreno (15)	
45	25 October 1953	7	**Real Madrid**	FC Barcelona	**5–0** (4–0)	di Stéfano (10, 85), Roque Olsen (34, 35), Molowny (39)	
46	21 February 1954	22	**FC Barcelona**	Real Madrid	**5–1** (1–1)	Tejada (14, 86), César (50), Moreno (74), Manchón (89)	di Stéfano (6)
47	21 November 1954	11	**Real Madrid**	FC Barcelona	**3–0** (1–0)	di Stéfano (p. 44), Héctor Rial (66), Joseito (67)	
48	6 March 1955	26	FC Barcelona	Real Madrid	**2–2** (1–1)	Basora (31), Dagoberto Moll (70)	Gento (19, 64)
49	13 November 1955	10	**Real Madrid**	FC Barcelona	**2–1** (1–0)	Héctor Rial (35), Marquitos (89)	Areta (77)

50	18 March 1956	25	**FC Barcelona**	Real Madrid	**2–0** (2–0)	Villaverde (18, 29)	
51	11 November 1956	10	**FC Barcelona**	Real Madrid	**1–0** (0–0)	Luis Suárez (46)	
52	3 March 1957	25	**Real Madrid**	FC Barcelona	**1–0** (1–0)	Joseito (21)	
53	13 October 1957	5	**Real Madrid**	FC Barcelona	**3–0** (2–0)	Kopa (10), Héctor Rial (43), di Stéfano (73)	
54	2 February 1958	20	FC Barcelona	**Real Madrid**	**0–2** (0–2)		Marsal (34), Héctor Rial (37)
55	26 October 1958	7	**FC Barcelona**	Real Madrid	**4–0** (1–0)	Evaristo (22, 68, 70), Tejada (84)	
56	15 February 1959	22	**Real Madrid**	FC Barcelona	**1–0** (0–0)	Herrera (79')	
57	29 November 1959	11	**Real Madrid**	FC Barcelona	**2–0** (1–0)	Mateos (5), di Stéfano (82)	
58	20 March 1960	26	**FC Barcelona**	Real Madrid	**3–1** (0–0)	Kocsis (50), Martínez (60), Villaverde (62)	di Stéfano (58)
59	4 December 1960	12	FC Barcelona	**Real Madrid**	**3–5** (2–3)	Martínez (28), Villaverde (34), Kubala (89)	di Stéfano (3, 81), del Sol (15), Gento (43, 79)
60	26 March 1961	27	**Real Madrid**	FC Barcelona	**3–2** (0–0)	del Sol (55), di Stéfano (60), Puskás (78)	Luis Suárez (80), Kubala (89)
61	30 September 1961	10	**Real Madrid**	FC Barcelona	**2–0** (1–0)	Puskás (14), del Sol (72)	
62	21 January 1962	20	**FC Barcelona**	Real Madrid	**3–1** (2–0)	Evaristo (4, 83), Kocsis (40)	Félix Ruiz (86)
63	30 September 1962	3	**Real Madrid**	FC Barcelona	**2–0** (1–0)	di Stéfano (20, 70)	
64	27 January 1963	18	FC Barcelona	**Real Madrid**	**1–5** (1–2)	Ré (34)	Puskás (p. 24, 35, 71), di Stéfano (47), Gento (67)
65	15 December 1963	12	**Real Madrid**	FC Barcelona	**4–0** (1–0)	Puskás (37, 68, p. 84), di Stéfano (77)	

66	30 March 1964	27	FC Barcelona	**Real Madrid**	**1–2** (1–2)	Zaldúa (27)	Gento (18), Puskás (43)
67	8 November 1964	9	**Real Madrid**	FC Barcelona	**4–1** (2–0)	Amancio (16, 31, 74), Serena (76)	Ré (68)
68	28 February 1965	24	FC Barcelona	**Real Madrid**	**1–2** (1–0)	Ré (40)	Pirri (63), Serena (70)
69	19 December 1965	14	Real Madrid	**FC Barcelona**	**1–3** (1–3)	Félix Ruiz (20)	Fusté (7, 8), Zaldúa (34)
70	27 March 1966	29	**FC Barcelona**	Real Madrid	**2–1** (0–1)	Rifé (59), Zaballa (63)	Gento (39)
71	20 November 1966	10	**Real Madrid**	FC Barcelona	**1–0** (0–0)	Fidalgo (89)	
72	19 March 1967	25	**FC Barcelona**	Real Madrid	**2–1** (1–1)	Fusté (7, 89)	Amancio (42)
73	10 December 1967	12	Real Madrid	FC Barcelona	**1–1** (0–0)	Gento (p. 65)	Zaldúa (78)
74	9 April 1968	27	FC Barcelona	Real Madrid	**1–1** (1–1)	Zaldúa (12)	Pirri (43)
75	16 November 1968	9	**Real Madrid**	FC Barcelona	**2–1** (1–1)	Pirri (32), José Luis (75)	Zaldúa (19)
76	9 March 1969	24	FC Barcelona	Real Madrid	**1–1** (1–0)	Zaldúa (26)	Gento (p. 87)
77	14 September 1969	1	Real Madrid	FC Barcelona	**3–3** (2–2)	Fleitas (18, 38), Gento (63)	Bustillo (3, 5), Rexach (71)
78	28 December 1969	16	**FC Barcelona**	Real Madrid	**1–0** (1–0)	Gallego (29)	
79	25 October 1970	7	Real Madrid	**FC Barcelona**	**0–1** (0–1)		Zabalza (28)
80	14 February 1971	22	FC Barcelona	**Real Madrid**	**0–1** (0–0)		Grande (67)
81	28 November 1971	11	Real Madrid	FC Barcelona	**1–1** (1–0)	Grosso (6)	Asensi (68)

82	3 April 1972	28	**FC Barcelona**	Real Madrid	**1–0** (1–0)	Asensi (11)	
83	1 October 1972	5	**FC Barcelona**	Real Madrid	**1–0** (0–0)	Barrios (52)	
84	25 February 1973	22	Real Madrid	FC Barcelona	**0–0** (0–0)		
85	7 October 1973	6	FC Barcelona	Real Madrid	**0–0** (0–0)		
86	17 February 1974	22	Real Madrid	**FC Barcelona**	**0–5** (0–2)		Asensi (30, 54), Cruijff (39), Pérez (65), Sotil (69)
87	5 January 1975	15	**Real Madrid**	FC Barcelona	**1–0** (1–0)	Roberto Martínez (43)	
88	11 May 1975	32	FC Barcelona	Real Madrid	**0–0** (0–0)		
89	28 December 1975	15	**FC Barcelona**	Real Madrid	**2–1** (1–0)	Neeskens (3), Rexach (89)	Pirri (64)
90	30 April 1976	32	Real Madrid	**FC Barcelona**	**0–2** (0–1)		Rexach (15), Heredia (64)
91	19 September 1976	3	**FC Barcelona**	Real Madrid	**3–1** (1–0)	Marcial (29), Cruyff (53), Heredia (86)	Pirri (52)
92	30 January 1977	20	Real Madrid	FC Barcelona	**1–1** (1–1)	Pirri (p. 2)	Cruyff (16)
93	4 December 1977	12	FC Barcelona	**Real Madrid**	**2–3** (1–2)	Jensen (23), Santillana (35), Stielike (54)	Rexach (p. 30, 67)
94	30 January 1978	29	**Real Madrid**	FC Barcelona	**4–0** (2–0)	Jensen (6, 10), Juanito (69), Santillana (80)	
95	23 September 1978	4	**Real Madrid**	FC Barcelona	**3–1** (2–1)	Santillana (29, 46), Jensen (32)	Neeskens (15)
96	17 February 1979	21	**FC Barcelona**	Real Madrid	**2–0** (0–0)	Krankl (52), Asensi (61)	
97	23 September 1979	3	**Real Madrid**	FC Barcelona	**3–2** (3–2)	Santillana (6), Juanito (8), Cunningham (32)	Landáburu (23), Krankl (36)
98	10 February 1980	20	FC Barcelona	**Real Madrid**	**0–2** (0–0)		García Hernández (61), Santillana (63)

99	30 November 1980	13	**FC Barcelona**	Real Madrid	**2–1** (1–1)	Schuster (15), Quini (64)	Juanito (22)
100	29 March 1981	30	**Real Madrid**	FC Barcelona	**3–0** (0–0)	Juanito (p. 53), Santillana (71), Stielike (76)	
101	20 December 1981	16	**FC Barcelona**	Real Madrid	**3–1** (1–0)	Alexanko (7), Quini (53, p. 60)	Juanito (49)
102	29 March 1982	30	**Real Madrid**	FC Barcelona	**3–1** (2–1)	Rafael Cortés (6), Stielike (p. 45), Isidro (82)	Quini (42)
103	27 November 1982	13	Real Madrid	**FC Barcelona**	**0–2** (0–1)		Esteban Vigo (14), Quini (86)
104	26 March 1983	30	**FC Barcelona**	Real Madrid	**2–1** (1–1)	Maradona (45), Perico Alonso (77)	Juanito (20)
105	22 October 1983	8	FC Barcelona	**Real Madrid**	**1–2** (1–2)	Quini (p. 17)	Juanito (p. 12), Santillana (20)
106	25 February 1984	25	**Real Madrid**	FC Barcelona	**2–1** (1–0)	Juanito (16), Santillana (80)	Maradona (56)
107	2 September 1984	1	Real Madrid	**FC Barcelona**	**0–3** (0–0)		Ángel (o.g.46), Archibald (86), Calderé (89)
108	30 December 1984	18	**FC Barcelona**	Real Madrid	**3–2** (1–1)	Gerardo (25), Migueli (53), Esteban Vigo (79)	Sanchís (30), Butragueño (89)
109	9 November 1985	11	**FC Barcelona**	Real Madrid	**2–0** (1–0)	Marcos Alonso (2), Calderé (72)	
110	8 March 1986	25	**Real Madrid**	FC Barcelona	**3–1** (0–0)	Maceda (64), Valdano (67), Butragueño (83)	Amarilla (51)
111	8 October 1986	8	Real Madrid	FC Barcelona	**1–1** (1–1)	Hugo Sánchez (p. 27)	Pedraza (6)
112	31 January 1987	25	**FC Barcelona**	Real Madrid	**3–2** (2–0)	Lineker (2, 5, 47)	Valdano (61), Hugo Sánchez (p. 80)
113	12 April 1987	35	Real Madrid	FC Barcelona	**0–0** (0–0)		
114	23 May 1987	40	**FC Barcelona**	Real Madrid	**2–1** (1–0)	Lineker (39), Roberto (p. 60)	Hugo Sánchez (53)
115	2 January 1988	16	**Real Madrid**	FC Barcelona	**2–1** (2–1)	Hugo Sánchez (p. 22, 41)	Schuster (p. 30)

116	30 April 1988	35	**FC Barcelona**	Real Madrid	**2–0** (1–0)	Carrasco (1), Lineker (70)	
117	22 October 1988	8	**Real Madrid**	FC Barcelona	**3–2** (0–1)	Hugo Sánchez (57), Aldana (59), Gordillo (81)	Bakero (21), Carrasco (70)
118	1 April 1989	27	FC Barcelona	Real Madrid	**0–0** (0–0)		
119	7 October 1989	6	**FC Barcelona**	Real Madrid	**3–1** (1–1)	Salinas (10), R.Koeman (p. 74, p. 89)	Hugo Sánchez (p. 5)
120	15 February 1990	25	**Real Madrid**	FC Barcelona	**3–2** (3–0)	Míchel (24), Butragueño (45), Hugo Sánchez (p. 46)	Salinas (21, 70)
121	19 January 1991	19	**FC Barcelona**	Real Madrid	**2–1** (1–1)	Laudrup (18), Spasić (o.g. 62)	Butragueño (28)
122	8 June 1991	38	**Real Madrid**	FC Barcelona	**1–0** (0–0)	Aldana (47)	
123	19 October 1991	6	Real Madrid	FC Barcelona	**1–1** (1–0)	Prosinečki (19)	R.Koeman (p. 58)
124	7 March 1992	25	FC Barcelona	Real Madrid	**1–1** (1–0)	R.Koeman (36)	Hierro (66)
125	5 September 1992	1	**FC Barcelona**	Real Madrid	**2–1** (1–0)	Bakero (4), Stoichkov (87)	Míchel (p. 71)
126	30 January 1993	20	**Real Madrid**	FC Barcelona	**2–1** (2–1)	Zamorano (9), Míchel (p. 41)	Amor (p. 15)
127	8 January 1994	18	**FC Barcelona**	Real Madrid	**5–0** (1–0)	Romário (24, 56, 81), Koeman (47), Iván Iglesias (86)	
128	7 May 1994	37	Real Madrid	**FC Barcelona**	**0–1** (0–0)		Amor (77)
129	7 January 1995	16	**Real Madrid**	FC Barcelona	**5–0** (3–0)	Zamorano (5, 21, 39), Luis Enrique (68), Amavisca (70)	
130	27 May 1995	35	**FC Barcelona**	Real Madrid	**1–0** (0–0)	Nadal (62)	
131	1 October 1995	5	Real Madrid	FC Barcelona	**1–1** (1–1)	Raúl (12)	Roger (31)
132	11 February 1996	26	**FC Barcelona**	Real Madrid	**3–0** (1–0)	Kodro (37, 93), Figo (71)	
133	8 December 1996	16	**Real Madrid**	FC Barcelona	**2–0** (1–0)	Suker (24), Mijatovic (48)	
134	11 May 1997	37	**FC Barcelona**	Real Madrid	**1–0** (1–0)	Ronaldo (45)	

135	2 November 1997	9	Real Madrid	**FC Barcelona**	**2–3** (0–1)	Raúl (48), Suker (61)	Rivaldo (5), Luis Enrique (51), Giovanni (85)
136	8 March 1998	28	**FC Barcelona**	Real Madrid	**3–0** (0–0)	Anderson (69), Figo (80), Giovanni (85)	
137	20 September 1998	3	Real Madrid	FC Barcelona	**2–2** (2–1)	Raúl (7, 37)	Kluivert (12), Anderson (83)
138	15 February 1999	22	**FC Barcelona**	Real Madrid	**3–0** (2–0)	Luis Enrique (4, 36), Rivaldo (80)	
139	14 October 1999	7	FC Barcelona	Real Madrid	**2–2** (1–1)	Rivaldo (28), Figo (50)	Raúl (26, 85)
140	27 February 2000	26	**Real Madrid**	FC Barcelona	**3–0** (2–0)	Roberto Carlos (5), Anelka (19), Morientes (52)	
141	22 October 2000	6	**FC Barcelona**	Real Madrid	**2–0** (1–0)	Luis Enrique (26), Simão (79)	
142	4 March 2001	25	Real Madrid	FC Barcelona	**2–2** (2–1)	Raúl (6, 36)	Rivaldo (35, 69)
143	5 November 2001	11	**Real Madrid**	FC Barcelona	**2–0** (1–0)	Morientes (23), Figo (92)	
144	17 March 2002	30	FC Barcelona	Real Madrid	**1–1** (0–1)	Xavi (58)	Zidane (38)
145	24 November 2002	11	FC Barcelona	Real Madrid	**0–0** (0–0)		
146	20 April 2003	30	Real Madrid	FC Barcelona	**1–1** (1–1)	Ronaldo (16)	Luis Enrique (32)
147	7 December 2003	15	FC Barcelona	**Real Madrid**	**1–2** (0–1)	Kluivert (83)	Roberto Carlos (37), Ronaldo (75)
148	25 April 2004	34	Real Madrid	**FC Barcelona**	**1–2** (0–0)	Solari (54)	Kluivert (58), Xavi (85)
149	20 November 2004	12	**FC Barcelona**	Real Madrid	**3–0** (2–0)	Eto'o (28), van Bronckhorst (42), Ronaldinho (p. 76)	
150	10 April 2005	31	**Real Madrid**	FC Barcelona	**4–2** (2–1)	Zidane (7), Ronaldo (20), Raúl (46), Owen (66)	Eto'o (29), Ronaldinho (73)
151	19 November 2005	12	Real Madrid	**FC Barcelona**	**0–3** (0–1)		Eto'o (14), Ronaldinho (59, 77)

152	1 April 2006	31	FC Barcelona	Real Madrid	**1–1** (1–1)	Ronaldinho (p. 20)	Ronaldo (36)
153	22 October 2006	7	**Real Madrid**	FC Barcelona	**2–0** (1–0)	Raúl (3), van Nistelrooy (50)	
154	10 March 2007	26	FC Barcelona	Real Madrid	**3–3** (2–2)	Messi (10, 27, 88)	van Nistelrooy (4, p. 12), Ramos (72)
155	23 December 2007	17	FC Barcelona	**Real Madrid**	**0–1** (0–1)		Baptista (36)
156	7 May 2008	34	**Real Madrid**	FC Barcelona	**4–1** (2–0)	Raúl (12), Robben (20), Higuaín (62), van Nistelrooy (p. 77)	Henry (86)
157	13 December 2008	17	**FC Barcelona**	Real Madrid	**2–0** (0–0)	Eto'o (83), Messi (90)	
158	2 May 2009	34	Real Madrid	**FC Barcelona**	**2–6** (1–3)	Higuaín (14), Ramos (56),	Henry (18, 58), Puyol (25), Messi (35, 75), Piqué (83)
159	29 November 2009	12	**FC Barcelona**	Real Madrid	**1–0** (0–0)	Ibrahimović (56)	
160	10 April 2010	31	Real Madrid	**FC Barcelona**	**0–2** (0–1)		Messi (33), Pedro (56)

Head-to-head results

Real Madrid wins	68
FC Barcelona wins	62
Draws	30
Total matches	160

Spanish Cup matches

Below are all of the Copa del Rey matches which Barcelona and Real Madrid have played against each other. Starting in 1901, the Copa Del Rey was the first nation-wide tournament in Spain before the establishment of La Liga in 1929.

Season	Round		Home team	Away team	Score (H/T)	Goals (home)	Goals (away)
1925	Quarter final	1st leg	Real Madrid	**FC Barcelona**	**1–5** (0–3)	Monjardín (47)	Samitier (19, 26 , 43), Piera (79)
		2nd leg	**FC Barcelona**	Real Madrid	**3–0** (2–0)	Piera (8), Samitier (18, 51)	
1935	Final		**Real Madrid**	FC Barcelona	**2–1** (2–1)	Eugenio (6), Lécue (12)	Escolà (29)
1942	Semi final	1st leg	**FC Barcelona**	Real Madrid	**3–0** (2–0)	Valle Mas (33), Escolà (p. 43), Sospedra (60)	
		2nd leg	**Real Madrid**	FC Barcelona	**11–1** (8-0)	Pruden (4), Barinaga (3), "Chus" Alonso (2), Alsúa and Botella	Martín
1953	Semi final	1st leg	**Real Madrid**	FC Barcelona	**1–0** (1–0)	Mateos (86)	
		2nd leg	**FC Barcelona**	Real Madrid	**3–1** (2–1)	César (9, 12), Biosca (87)	Pérez Payá (24)
1956	Quarter final	1st leg	Real Madrid	FC Barcelona	**2–2** (2–1)	di Stéfano (p. 20, 35)	Kubala (14), Basora (53)
		2nd leg	**FC Barcelona**	Real Madrid	**6–1** (2–0)	Martínez (4, 48, 50, 63), Kubala (35), Villaverde (79)	Olivella (o.g. 75)
1958	Quarter final	1st leg	Real Madrid	**FC Barcelona**	**2–4** (2–0)	Puskas (20), Mateos (35)	Kocsic (51, 69), Luis Suárez (67, 71)
		2nd leg	**FC Barcelona**	Real Madrid	**3–1** (2–1)	Luis Suárez (p. 34, 44), Villaverde (63)	Gento (36)
1961	Quarter final	1st leg	Real Madrid	**FC Barcelona**	**0–1** (0–0)		Martínez (62)
		2nd leg	FC Barcelona	**Real Madrid**	**1–3** (0–0)	Pereda (85)	Del Sol (65), Puskas (83), Gento (90)
1967–68	Final		**FC Barcelona**	Real Madrid	**1–0** (1–0)	Zunzunegui (o.g. 6)	
1969–70	Quarter final	1st leg	**Real Madrid**	FC Barcelona	**2–0** (2–0)	Grosso (5), Amancio (44)	
		2nd leg	FC Barcelona	Real Madrid	**1–1** (1–0)	Rexach (45)	Amancio (p. 60)

1973–74	Final		**Real Madrid**	FC Barcelona	**4–0** (1–0)	Santillana (6), Rubiñán (47), Aguilar (50), Pirri (83)	
1982–83	Final		**FC Barcelona**	Real Madrid	**2–1** (1–0)	Víctor (32), Marcos (90)	Santillana (50)
1989–90	Final		**FC Barcelona**	Real Madrid	**2–0** (0–0)	Amor (68), Julio Salinas (90)	
1992–93	Semi final	1st leg	Real Madrid	FC Barcelona	**1–1** (1–1)	Zamorano (40)	Bakero (30)
		2nd leg	FC Barcelona	**Real Madrid**	**1–2** (0–1)	Laudrup (87)	Míchel (p.24), Zamorano (82)
1996–97	Last 16	1st leg	**FC Barcelona**	Real Madrid	**3–2** (1–1)	Ronaldo (13), Miguel Nadal (70), Giovanni (79)	Šuker (16), Hierro (67)
		2nd leg	Real Madrid	FC Barcelona	**1–1** (0–0)	Šuker (p. 80)	Roberto Carlos (o.g. 69)

League Cup matches

The Copa de la Liga was a tournament created in 1982, but low support from the participating clubs saw it disbanded four years later.

Season	Round		Home team	Away team	Score (H/T)	Goals (home)	Goals (away)
1982–83	Final	1st leg	Real Madrid	FC Barcelona	**2–2** (0–0)	del Bosque (63), Juanito (69)	Carrasco (50), Maradona (57)
		2nd leg	**FC Barcelona**	Real Madrid	**2–1** (0–0)	Maradona (19), Alexanko (20)	Santillana (84)
1984–85	Quarter final	1st leg	FC Barcelona	Real Madrid	**2–2** (2–0)	Clos (40), Marcos (44)	Valdano (67), Juanito (75)
		2nd leg	Real Madrid	FC Barcelona	**1–1** (0–0)	Valdano (83)	Moratalla (57)
1985–86	Last 16	1st leg	FC Barcelona	Real Madrid	**2–2** (1–1)	Clos (24), Archibald (50)	Pardeza (36), Cholo (52)
		2nd leg	Real Madrid	**FC Barcelona**	**0–4** (0–2)		Amarilla (2, 41), Urbano (47), Esteban (67)

Spanish Super Cup matches

The Supercopa de España is a Spanish football championship contested by the winners of the La Liga and the Copa del Rey. Established in 1982, it is the Spanish equivalent to the English FA Community Shield, where the winners of the FA Premier League and FA Cup compete for the trophy.

Season		Home team	Away team	Score (H/T)	Goals (home)	Goals (away)
1988–89	1st leg	**Real Madrid**	FC Barcelona	**2–0** (0–0)	Míchel (71), Hugo Sánchez (78)	
	2nd leg	**FC Barcelona**	Real Madrid	**2–1** (1–1)	Bakero (37, 77)	Butragueño (14)
1990–91	1st leg	FC Barcelona	**Real Madrid**	**0–1** (0–0)		Míchel (54)
	2nd leg	**Real Madrid**	FC Barcelona	**4–1** (2–1)	Butragueño (21, 44), Hugo Sánchez (56), Aragón (70)	Goikoetxea (20)
1993–94	1st leg	**Real Madrid**	FC Barcelona	**3–1** (1–1)	Alfonso (35, 89) Zamorano (55)	Stoichkov (17)
	2nd leg	FC Barcelona	Real Madrid	**1–1** (0–1)	Bakero (65)	Zamorano (21)
1997–98	1st leg	**FC Barcelona**	Real Madrid	**2–1** (1–1)	Giovanni (1), Miguel Nadal (85)	Raúl (4)
	2nd leg	**Real Madrid**	FC Barcelona	**4–1** (1–0)	Raúl (42, 54), Mijatović (58), Seedorf (65)	Giovanni (80)

European Cup matches

The most prestigious tournament in Europe, Barcelona and Real Madrid has faced each other on several occasions in the European Cup, from 1992 onwards known as the Champions League.

Season	Round		Home team	Away team	Score (H/T)	Goals (home)	Goals (away)
1959–60	Semi final	1st leg	**Real Madrid**	FC Barcelona	**3–1** (2–1)	di Stéfano (17, 84), Puskás (28)	Martínez (37)
		2nd leg	FC Barcelona	**Real Madrid**	**1–3** (0–1)	Kocsis (89)	Puskás (25, 75), Gento (68)
1960–61	First round	1st leg	Real Madrid	FC Barcelona	**2–2** (2–1)	Mateos (1), Gento (33)	Luis Suárez (27, p. 88)
		2nd leg	**FC Barcelona**	Real Madrid	**2–1** (1–0)	Vergés (33), Evaristo (81)	Canário (87)

2001–2002	Semi final	1st leg	FC Barcelona	**Real Madrid**	**0–2** (0–0)		Zidane (55), McManaman (92)
		2nd leg	Real Madrid	FC Barcelona	**1–1** (1–0)	Raúl (43)	Helguera (o.g. 49)

All-time top scorers

From the previous tables the top 20 scorers are deduced. Players still active in La Liga marked with **bold**.

Rank	Nationality	Player	Liga	Cup	Super Cup	League Cup	Europe	Total
1	Argentina	Alfredo di Stéfano	14	2			2	**18**
2	Spain	Raúl	11		3		1	**15**
3	Spain	César	12	2				**14**
	Spain	Francisco Gento	10	2			2	**14**
	Hungary	Ferenc Puskás	9	2			3	**14**
6	Spain	Santillana	9	2		1		**12**
7	Mexico	Hugo Sánchez	8		2			**10**
	Spain	Juanito	8			2		**10**
9	Spain	Estanislao Basora	8	1				**9**
	Spain	Josep Samitier	4	5				**9**
11	Spain	Jaime Lazcano	8					**8**
	Spain	Luis Suárez	2	4			2	**8**
	Chile	Iván Zamorano	4	2	2			**8**
	Paraguay	Eulogio Martínez	2	5			1	**8**
	Spain	Santiago Bernabéu		8				**8**
16	Argentina	**Lionel Messi**	7					**7**
	Brazil	Ronaldo	6	1				**7**
	Spain	Pahiño	7					**7**
	Spain	Pirri	6	1				**7**
	Spain	Josep Escolà	5	2				**7**
	Spain	Sabino Barinaga	4	3				**7**

Players who played for both clubs

While the transfers of Luis Enrique from Real Madrid to Barcelona and Luís Figo from Barcelona to Real Madrid caused an uproar amongst the fans of their respective clubs, the rivalry between the two teams has not prevented players from switching teams, sometimes without controversy.[citation needed]

- Alfonso Albéniz (Barça to Madrid) (1902)
- Luciano Lizarraga (Madrid to Barça) (1905)
- Charles Wallace (Barça to Madrid) (1906)
- José Quirante (Barça to Madrid) (1906)
- Alfonso Albéniz (Barça to Madrid) (1911)
- Arsenio Comamala (Barça to Real Madrid) (1911)
- Walter Rozitsky (Barça to Madrid) (1913)
- Ricardo Zamora (Barça to Espanyol to Madrid) (1930)
- Josep Samitier (Barça to Madrid) (1932)
- Hilario Juan Marrero Pérez (Madrid to Valencia to Barça) (1939)
- Alfonso Navarro (Barça to Madrid) (1950)
- Justo Tejada (Barça to Madrid) (1961)
- Jesús María Pereda (Real Madrid to Real Valladolid to Sevilla to Barça) (1961)
- Evaristo de Macedo (Barça to Madrid) (1962)
- Fernand Goyvaerts (Barça to Madrid) (1965)
- Lucien Muller (Madrid to Barça) (1965)
- Lorenzo Amador (Madrid to Hércules CF to Barça) (1980)
- Bernd Schuster (Barça to Madrid) (1988)
- Luis Milla (Barça to Madrid) (1990)
- Gheorghe Hagi (Madrid to Brescia to Barça) (1991)
- Fernando "Nando" Muñoz (Barça to Madrid) (1992)
- Julen Lopetegui (Madrid to CD Logroñés to Barça) (1994)
- Michael Laudrup (Barça to Madrid) (1994)
- Robert Prosinečki (Madrid to Real Oviedo to Barça) (1995)
- Miquel Soler (Barça to Sevilla to Madrid) (1995)
- Luis Enrique (Madrid to Barça) (1996)
- Daniel García Lara (Madrid to Real Mallorca to Barça) (1999)
- Luís Figo (Barça to Madrid) (2000)
- Albert Celades (Barça to Celta Vigo to Real Madrid) (2000)
- Alfonso Pérez (Madrid to Real Betis to Barça) (2000)
- Ronaldo (Barça to Internazionale to Madrid) (2002)
- Samuel Eto'o (Madrid to Real Mallorca to Barça) (2004)
- Javier Saviola (Barça to Madrid) (2007)

See also

- Major football rivalries
- Sports rivalry
- Nationalism and sport

Notes

General

- Ball, Phill (2003). *Morbo: The Story of Spanish Football*. WSC Books Limited. ISBN 0954013468.
- Farred, Grant (2008). *Long distance love: a passion for football*. Temple University Press. ISBN 1592133746.

Specific

El Derbi madrileño

El Derbi madrileño (English: *Madrid Derby*) is the name given to football matches between Real Madrid and Atlético Madrid, both of them from Madrid, Spain.

Real Madrid and Atletico are clubs with contrasting identities and very different fates - a divide similar to the Manchester derby, but far more political. Historically, Real Madrid have long been seen as the establishment club. On the other side, Atletico was always characterized by a 'sentimiento de rebeldía' (a sense of rebellion) although, during the early Franco years, it was Atlético that was the preferred team of the regime, being associated with the military airforce, until the regime's preferences moved towards Real Madrid in the 1950s. Franco sought to make political capital out of Real Madrid's European Cup titles at a time when Spain was internationally isolated - "Real Madrid are the best embassy we ever had", said one minister. Thus, Atleti fans regularly chanted that Real was *"el equipo del gobierno, la verguenza del país"*--the team of the government, the shame of the country--and adopted a more left-wing slant (tempered by the rise of ultras culture and Rayo Vallecano's presence as the "true" leftist club) to combat the conservative Real fanbase. Bernabeu, Real Madrid's stadium, is majestic, alongside banks and businesses on the classy and aristocratic Castellana, while Calderon can be found beside a brewery along the river; Real Madrid draw greater support because of its successes, while Atletico has a more working class fan base, which comes particularly from the south of the city.

Matches

These are only the league matches

Season	Home	Away	Home	Away
1928-1929	**Real Madrid** 2	Atlético Madrid 1	Atlético Madrid 0	**Real Madrid** 3
1929-1930	**Real Madrid** 4	Atlético Madrid 1	**Atlético Madrid** 2	Real Madrid 1
1935-1936	**Real Madrid** 2	Atlético Madrid 0	Atlético Madrid 2	Real Madrid 2
1936-1937	No matches because of the Spanish Civil War			
1937-1938				
1938-1939				
1939-1940	**Real Madrid** 2	Atlético Madrid 0	**Atlético Madrid** 2	Real Madrid 1
1940-1941	Real Madrid 1	**Atlético Madrid** 3	**Atlético Madrid** 4	Real Madrid 1
1941-1942	**Real Madrid** 4	Atlético Madrid 1	**Atlético Madrid** 2	Real Madrid 0
1942-1943	Real Madrid 1	**Atlético Madrid** 3	**Atlético Madrid** 2	Real Madrid 1
1943-1944	**Real Madrid** 3	Atlético Madrid 2	**Atlético Madrid** 3	Real Madrid 1
1944-1945	**Real Madrid** 3	Atlético Madrid 1	Atlético Madrid 0	**Real Madrid** 1
1945-1946	**Real Madrid** 2	Atlético Madrid 1	**Atlético Madrid** 3	Real Madrid 1
1946-1947	Real Madrid 1	**Atlético Madrid** 2	Atlético Madrid 2	**Real Madrid** 3
1947-1948	Real Madrid 1	Atlético Madrid 1	**Atlético Madrid** 5	Real Madrid 0
1948-1949	Real Madrid 1	**Atlético Madrid** 2	Atlético Madrid 0	**Real Madrid** 2
1949-1950	**Real Madrid** 4	Atlético Madrid 2	**Atlético Madrid** 5	Real Madrid 1
1950-1951	Real Madrid 3	**Atlético Madrid** 6	**Atlético Madrid** 4	Real Madrid 0
1951-1952	**Real Madrid** 2	Atlético Madrid 1	**Atlético Madrid** 3	Real Madrid 2

1952-1953	**Real Madrid** 2	Atlético Madrid 0	Atlético Madrid 1	**Real Madrid** 2
1953-1954	**Real Madrid** 2	Atlético Madrid 1	Atlético Madrid 3	**Real Madrid** 4
1954-1955	**Real Madrid** 1	Atlético Madrid 0	Atlético Madrid 2	**Real Madrid** 4
1955-1956	**Real Madrid** 3	Atlético Madrid 2	**Atlético Madrid** 1	Real Madrid 0
1956-1957	**Real Madrid** 0	Atlético Madrid 2	Atlético Madrid 2	**Real Madrid** 4
1957-1958	Real Madrid 0	Atlético Madrid 0	Atlético Madrid 1	Real Madrid 1
1958-1959	**Real Madrid** 5	Atlético Madrid 0	**Atlético Madrid** 2	Real Madrid 1
1959-1960	**Real Madrid** 3	Atlético Madrid 2	Atlético Madrid 3	Real Madrid 3
1960-1961	**Real Madrid** 3	Atlético Madrid 1	**Atlético Madrid** 1	Real Madrid 0
1961-1962	**Real Madrid** 2	Atlético Madrid 1	**Atlético Madrid** 1	Real Madrid 0
1962-1963	**Real Madrid** 4	Atlético Madrid 3	Atlético Madrid 1	Real Madrid 1
1963-1964	**Real Madrid** 5	Atlético Madrid 1	Atlético Madrid 0	**Real Madrid** 1
1964-1965	Real Madrid 0	**Atlético Madrid** 1	Atlético Madrid 0	**Real Madrid** 1
1965-1966	**Real Madrid** 3	Atlético Madrid 1	Atlético Madrid 1	Real Madrid 1
1966-1967	**Real Madrid** 2	Atlético Madrid 1	Atlético Madrid 2	Real Madrid 2
1967-1968	Real Madrid 0	Atlético Madrid 0	Atlético Madrid 1	Real Madrid 1
1968-1969	Real Madrid 0	Atlético Madrid 0	Atlético Madrid 0	**Real Madrid** 1
1969-1970	Real Madrid 1	Atlético Madrid 1	**Atlético Madrid** 3	Real Madrid 0
1970-1971	**Real Madrid** 1	Atlético Madrid 0	Atlético Madrid 2	Real Madrid 2
1971-1972	**Real Madrid** 1	Atlético Madrid 0	**Atlético Madrid** 4	Real Madrid 1

1972-1973	Real Madrid 0	**Atlético Madrid** 1	Atlético Madrid 1	**Real Madrid** 2
1973-1974	**Real Madrid** 2	Atlético Madrid 0	Atlético Madrid 0	**Real Madrid** 2
1974-1975	**Real Madrid** 1	Atlético Madrid 0	Atlético Madrid 1	Real Madrid 1
1975-1976	**Real Madrid** 1	Atlético Madrid 0	**Atlético Madrid** 1	Real Madrid 0
1976-1977	Real Madrid 1	Atlético Madrid 1	**Atlético Madrid** 4	Real Madrid 0
1977-1978	**Real Madrid** 4	Atlético Madrid 2	Atlético Madrid 1	**Real Madrid** 3
1978-1979	Real Madrid 1	Atlético Madrid 1	Atlético Madrid 2	Real Madrid 2
1979-1980	**Real Madrid** 4	Atlético Madrid 0	Atlético Madrid 1	Real Madrid 1
1980-1981	**Real Madrid** 2	Atlético Madrid 0	**Atlético Madrid** 3	Real Madrid 1
1981-1982	**Real Madrid** 2	Atlético Madrid 1	Atlético Madrid 2	**Real Madrid** 3
1982-1983	**Real Madrid** 3	Atlético Madrid 1	Atlético Madrid 0	Real Madrid 0
1983-1984	**Real Madrid** 5	Atlético Madrid 0	**Atlético Madrid** 1	Real Madrid 0
1984-1985	Real Madrid 0	**Atlético Madrid** 4	Atlético Madrid 0	**Real Madrid** 1
1985-1986	**Real Madrid** 2	Atlético Madrid 1	Atlético Madrid 0	**Real Madrid** 1
1986-1987	**Real Madrid** 4	Atlético Madrid 1	Atlético Madrid 1	Real Madrid 1
1987-1988	Real Madrid 0	**Atlético Madrid** 4	Atlético Madrid 1	**Real Madrid** 3
1988-1989	**Real Madrid** 2	Atlético Madrid 1	Atlético Madrid 3	Real Madrid 3
1989-1990	**Real Madrid** 3	Atlético Madrid 1	Atlético Madrid 3	Real Madrid 3
1990-1991	Real Madrid 0	**Atlético Madrid** 3	Atlético Madrid 0	**Real Madrid** 3
1991-1992	**Real Madrid** 3	Atlético Madrid 2	**Atlético Madrid** 2	Real Madrid 0

1992-1993	**Real Madrid** 1	Atlético Madrid 0	Atlético Madrid 1	Real Madrid 1
1993-1994	**Real Madrid** 1	Atlético Madrid 0	Atlético Madrid 0	Real Madrid 0
1994-1995	**Real Madrid** 4	Atlético Madrid 2	Atlético Madrid 0	**Real Madrid** 2
1995-1996	**Real Madrid** 1	Atlético Madrid 0	Atlético Madrid 1	**Real Madrid** 2
1996-1997	**Real Madrid** 3	Atlético Madrid 1	Atlético Madrid 1	**Real Madrid** 4
1997-1998	Real Madrid 1	Atlético Madrid 1	Atlético Madrid 1	Real Madrid 1
1998-1999	**Real Madrid** 4	Atlético Madrid 2	**Atlético Madrid** 3	Real Madrid 1
1999-2000	Real Madrid 1	**Atlético Madrid** 3	Atlético Madrid 1	Real Madrid 1
2000-2001	No matches because of Atlético in Spanish Second Division			
2001-2002				
2002-2003	Real Madrid 2	Atlético Madrid 2	Atlético Madrid 0	**Real Madrid** 4
2003-2004	**Real Madrid** 2	Atlético Madrid 0	Atlético Madrid 1	**Real Madrid** 2
2004-2005	Real Madrid 0	Atlético Madrid 0	Atlético Madrid 0	**Real Madrid** 3
2005-2006	**Real Madrid** 2	Atlético Madrid 1	Atlético Madrid 0	**Real Madrid** 3
2006-2007	Real Madrid 1	Atlético Madrid 1	Atlético Madrid 1	Real Madrid 1
2007-2008	**Real Madrid** 2	Atlético Madrid 1	Atlético Madrid 0	**Real Madrid** 2
2008-2009	Real Madrid 1	Atlético Madrid 1	Atlético Madrid 1	**Real Madrid** 2
2009-2010	**Real Madrid** 3	Atlético Madrid 2	Atlético Madrid 2	**Real Madrid** 3

Head to head

Team	Win	Draw	Loss	Goals for
Real Madrid	79	31	35	260
Atlético Madrid	35	31	79	197

Players who played for both sides

- Luis Aragonés
- José Luis Caminero
- Rodrigo Fabri
- José Antonio García Calvo
- Juanito
- José Manuel Jurado
- José María Movilla
- José Antonio Reyes
- Hugo Sánchez
- Bernd Schuster
- Santiago Solari

See also

- Major football rivalries
- El Clásico
- Old Firm
- Sports rivalry
- Nationalism and sport

External links

- Official La Liga Web Site [1] (Spanish)

Real Madrid and Soccer Trivia

2010–11 Real Madrid C.F. season

2010–11 season	
Manager	José Mourinho
President	Florentino Pérez
La Liga	*3rd*
Copa del Rey	*Round of 32*
UEFA Champions League	*Group Stage*
Top goalscorer	League: Ronaldo (3) All: Three players tied (3)
Highest home attendance	70,000 vs Espanyol (21 September 2010)
Lowest home attendance	67,000 vs Deportivo (3 October 2010)

Home colours	**Away colours**	**Third colours**

← 2009–10 *2011–12* →

The **2010–11 season** is **Real Madrid Club de Fútbol**'s 80th season in La Liga. This article shows player statistics and all matches (official and friendly) that the club have and will play during the 2010–11 season.

Players

Squad information

N	P	Nat.	Name	Age	EU	Since	App	Goals	Ends	Transfer fee	Notes
1	GK		Casillas (*C*)	29	EU	1999	526	0	2017	Youth system	
2	CB		Carvalho	32	EU	2010	7	1	2012	€ 8M	
3	CB		Pepe	28	EU	2007	74	2	2012	€30M	Second nationality: Brazil
4	RB		Sergio Ramos (*VC*)	25	EU	2005	218	28	2013	€28M	
5	CM		Gago	25	EU	2007 Winter	114	1	2013	€20M	Second nationality: Italy
6	DM		Diarra	29	EU	2006	115	3	2011	€26M	
7	RW		Ronaldo	26	EU	2009	43	36	2015	€94M	
8	AM		Kaká	28	EU	2009	33	9	2015	€65M	Second nationality: Italy
9	CF		Benzema	23	EU	2009	39	10	2015	€35M	
10	DM		Lass	26	EU	2008 Winter	57	1	2013	€20M	
11	CM		Granero	23	EU	2009	39	3	2013	€ 4.5M	
12	LB		Marcelo (*VC2*)	22	Non-EU	2007 Winter	120	8	2015	€ 6.5M	
13	GK		Adán	23	EU	2009	0	0	2014	Youth system	
14	CM		Alonso	29	EU	2009	49	3	2014	€30M	
15	CB		Mateos	23	EU	2010	0	0	2014	Youth system	
16	AM		Canales	20	EU	2010	2	0	2016	€ 4.5M	
17	RB		Arbeloa	28	EU	2009	43	2	2014	€ 4.5M	
18	CB		R. Albiol	25	EU	2009	43	1	2014	€15M	
19	CB		Garay	24	Non-EU	2008	23	1	2014	€10M	
20	CF		Higuaín	23	EU	2007 Winter	147	67	2016	€13M	Second nationality: France
21	RW		P. León	24	EU	2010	3	0	2016	€10M	
22	LW		di María	23	EU	2010	8	3	2016	€25M	Second nationality: Italy

23	AM		Özil	22	EU	2010	8	1	2016	€18M	
24	DM		Khedira	24	EU	2010	8	0	2016	€12M	
25	GK		Dudek	38	EU	2007	10	0	2011	€12M	
26	LW		Juan Carlos	21	EU	2010	1	0		Youth system	

Last updated: 3 October 2010

Source: Realmadrid.com [1], Players transfer, Wikipedia players' articles, ESPN [2] (for appearances and goals), Realmadrid [3] (for player's number) and soccer-spain.com [4], sportec.es [5], footballdatabase [6] (for EU passport) and transfermarkt.co.uk [7] (for contracts)Ordered by position on pitch.

Transfers

In

N	P	Nat.	Name	Age	EU	Moving from	Type	Transfer window	Ends	Transfer fee	Source
16	AM		Canales	19	EU	Racing Santander	Transfer	Summer	2016	€ 4.5M	Realmadrid.com [8]
22	LW		di María	22	EU	Benfica	Transfer	Summer	2016	€25M	Realmadrid.com [9]
21	RW		P. León	23	EU	Getafe	Transfer	Summer	2016	€10M	Realmadrid.com [10]
24	DM		Khedira	23	EU	Stuttgart	Transfer	Summer	2016	€12M	Realmadrid.com [11]
2	CB		Carvalho	32	EU	Chelsea	Transfer	Summer	2012	€ 8M	Realmadrid.com [12]
23	AM		Özil	21	EU	Werder Bremen	Transfer	Summer	2016	€15M	Realmadrid.com [13]
15	CB		Mateos	23	EU	Youth system	Promoted	Summer		Youth system	Realmadrid.com [14]

Total spending: ▼ €74.5 million

Out

N	P	Nat.	Name	Age	EU	Moving to	Type	Transfer window	Transfer fee	Source
21	DF		Metzelder	29	EU	Schalke 04	End of contract	Summer	Free	Schalke04.de [15]
14	MF		Guti	33	EU	Beşiktaş	Contract cancellation	Summer	Free	BeşiktaşJK.com [16]
7	SS		Raúl	33	EU	Schalke 04	Contract cancellation	Summer	Free	Schalke04.de [17]
15	LM		Drenthe	23	EU	Hércules	Loan	Summer	N/A	Realmadrid.com [18]
23	AM		van der Vaart	27	EU	Tottenham Hotspur	Transfer	Summer	€11M	tottenhamhotspur.com [19]

Total income: ▲ €11 million

Long-term injury list

Date	Player	Injury	Estimated Return Date
August 2010	Kaká	Inflammation of cartilage in left knee	January 2011

Last updated: 8 August 2010

Source: Realmadrid.com [20]

Statistics

Squad statistics

	Total	La Liga	UEFA Champions League	Copa del Rey

N	P	Name	Nat.	GS	App	⚽	Min	App	⚽	App	⚽	App	⚽	Notes
1	GK	Casillas		8	8		756	6		2				
4	RB	Sergio Ramos		7	7		663	6		1				+ Source [21]
2	CB	Carvalho		7	7	1	662	6	1	1				
3	CB	Pepe		6	6	1	530	4	1	2				
12	LB	Marcelo		8	8		756	6		2				
14	CM	Alonso		8	8		747	6		2				
24	DM	Khedira		6	8		573	6		2				
7	SS	Ronaldo		8	8	3	756	6	3	2				
23	AM	Özil		6	8	1	523	6	1	2				
22	LW	di María		6	8	3	450	6	2	2	1			
20	CF	Higuaín		8	8	3	727	6	2	2	1			
17	RB	Arbeloa		4	5		386	3		2				
9	CF	Benzema		2	6	1	216	5	1	1				
10	DM	Lass		3	6		337	4		2				
16	AM	Canales		1	2		62	1		1				
21	RW	P. León			3		69	2		1				+ Source [22]
11	CM	Granero			3		41	3						
26	LW	Juan Carlos			1		12	1						
6	DM	Diarra			1		8			1				
5	CM	Gago												+ Source [23]
8	AM	Kaká												+ Source [24]
13	GK	Adán												
15	CB	Mateos												
18	CB	R. Albiol												
19	CB	Garay												+ Source [25]
25	GK	Dudek												

Last updated: 3 October 2010

Source: Match reports in competitive matches, Realmadrid.com [26], LFP.com [27] Soccernet.espn [28], sportec.es [29]

Ordered by start team, game starts and position on pitch (from back right to front left)

0 shown as blank

Top scorers

R	Player	Position	League	Champions League	Copa del Rey	Total
1	Higuaín	CF	2	1	0	3
	di María	LW	2	1	0	3
	Ronaldo	RW	3	0	0	3
2	Benzema	CF	1	0	0	1
	Pepe	CB	1	0	0	1
	Carvalho	CB	1	0	0	1
	Özil	AM	1	0	0	1

Top assister

R	Player	Position	League	Champions League	Copa del Rey	Total
1	Özil	AM	2	2	0	4
2	Ronaldo	RW	3	0	0	3
3	Higuaín	CF	2	0	0	2
4	Lass	DM	1	0	0	1
	Alonso	CM	1	0	0	1
	di María	LW	1	0	0	1

Last updated: 5 October 2010

Disciplinary record

N	P	Nat.	Name	Y	YY	R	Notes
3	CB		Pepe	1	1		
4	RB		Sergio Ramos	3			
14	CM		Alonso	2			
12	LB		Marcelo	2			
7	RW		Ronaldo	2			
11	CM		Granero	1			
2	CB		Carvalho	1			
22	LW		di María	1			
10	DM		Lass	1			

Last updated: 28 Sep 2010

Source: Competitive matches and LFP.com [30], sportec.es [31]

Only competitive matches

Y = Number of bookings; YY = Number of sending offs after a second yellow card; R = Number of sending offs by a direct red card..

Start formations

Qnt	Formation	Match(es)
6	4–2–3–1	2–6,8
2	4–3–3	1,7

Source: Match reports in Competitive matches Only competitive matches.

Starting 11

N	P	Nat.	Name	GS	Notes
1	GK		Casillas	8	
4	RB		Sergio Ramos	7	Also played as CB
2	CB		Carvalho	7	
3	CB		Pepe	6	
12	LB		Marcelo	8	
24	DM		Khedira	6	
14	DM		Alonso	8	
23	AM		Özil	6	
7	RW		Ronaldo	8	Also played as LW
22	LW		di María	6	Also played as RW
20	CF		Higuaín	8	

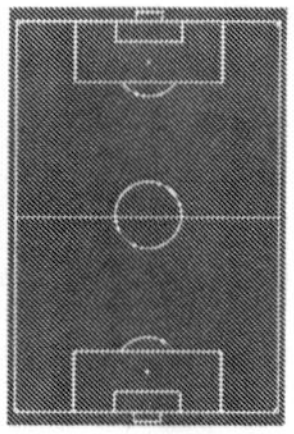

Casillas

Ramos

Pepe

Carvalho

Marcelo

Alonso

Khedira

Özil

Ronaldo

di María

Higuaín

Last updated: 3 October 2010

Source: Squad statistics and Start formations.

Only competitive matches.

Using the most used start formation.

Ordered by position on pitch (from back right to front left).

Overall

	Total	Home	Away
Games played	8	4	4
Games won	6	4	2
Games drawn	2	0	2
Games lost	0	0	0
Biggest win	6–1 vs Deportivo	6–1 vs Deportivo	2–1 vs Real Sociedad 1–0 vs Auxerre
Biggest loss			
Biggest win (League)	6–1 vs Deportivo	6-1 vs Deportivo	2–1 vs Real Sociedad
Biggest win (Cup)			
Biggest win (Europe)	2–0 vs Ajax	2–0 vs Ajax	1–0 vs Auxerre
Biggest loss (League)			
Biggest loss (Cup)			
Biggest loss (Europe)			
Clean sheets	6	3	3
Goals scored	15	12	3
Goals conceded	2	1	1
Goal difference	+13	+11	+2
Average GF per game	1.88	3	0.75
Average GA per game	0.25	0.25	0.25
Yellow cards	14	5	9
Red cards	1	1	0
Most appearances	(0)	–	
Most minutes played	(0)	–	
Top scorer	Higuaín di María Ronaldo (3)	–	
Top assister	Özil (4)	–	
Points	20/24 (83.33%)	12/12 (100%)	8/12 (66.67%)
Winning rate	75%	100%	50%

Last updated: 3 October 2010

Source: Competitive matches

Club

Coaching staff

Position	Staff
Head coach	José Mourinho
Assistant Coach	Aitor Karanka
Fitness Trainer	Rui Faria
Goalkeeper Coach	Silvino Louro
Technical Assistant	José Morais

Source: [1]

Kit

Supplier: Adidas
Sponsor: bwin.com

Home Away Third

Source: "The new shirt of Real Madrid 2010/11" [32]. Realmadrid.com. http://www.realmadrid.com/cs/Satellite/en/ 1202774162654/ noticia/ Especiales/ The_new_shirt_of_Real_Madrid_2010_11. htm. Retrieved 4 August 2010.
"Real Madrid Home Jersey" [33]. Adidas.com. http:/ / www. adidas. com/ campaigns/ football/ content/ products-detail.aspx?article=P96163&collection=clubs. Retrieved 4 August 2010.
"Real Madrid UEFA Champions League Away Shirt 2010/11" [34]. Realmadridshop.com. http://www.realmadridshop.com/stores/realmadrid/products/kit_selector.aspx?selectorid=317&lid=1. Retrieved 10 September 2010.

Other information

President	Florentino Pérez
Honorary Life President	Alfredo di Stéfano
1st Vice-president	Fernando Fernández Tapias
2nd Vice-president	Eduardo Fernández de Blas
Secretary of the Board	Enrique Sánchez González
Director General	Jorge Valdano
Director General of the President's Office	Manuel Redondo
Director of Institutional Relations	Emilio Butragueño
Advisor to the President	Zinedine Zidane
Sporting Director	Miguel Pardeza
Director of the Social Area	José Luis Sánchez
Director of the Legal Advisory Board	Javier López Farre
Ground (capacity and dimensions)	Santiago Bernabéu (80,354 / 105x68m)
Training ground	Ciudad Real Madrid

Source: Board of Directors (Realmadrid) [2], El club más laureado del mundo [35]

Competitions

Overall

Competition	Started round	Current position / round	Final position / round	First match	Last match
La Liga	—	3rd		29 August 2010	22 May 2011
UEFA Champions League	Group stage	—		15 September 2010	
Copa del Rey	Round of 32	—		27 October 2010	

Last updated: 3 October 2010 18:55 (CEST)

Source: Competitions' Wikipedia articles.

La Liga

Standings

Pos	Team	Pld	W	D	L	GF	GA	GD	Pts	Qualification or relegation
2	Villarreal	6	5	0	1	12	4	+8	**15**	2011–12 UEFA Champions League Group stage
3	Real Madrid	6	4	2	0	12	2	+10	**14**	
4	Barcelona	6	4	1	1	10	5	+5	**13**	2011–12 UEFA Champions League Play-off round

Updated to games played on 3 October 2010

Source: Yahoo! Sport [36]

Rules for classification:1st points; 2nd head-to-head points; 3rd head-to-head goal difference; 4th head-to-head goals scored; 5th goal difference; 6th number of goals scored; 7th Fair-play points (ascending order).

(C) = Champion; **(R)** = Relegated; **(P)** = Promoted; **(O)** = Play-off winner; **(A)** = Advances to a further round.

Only applicable when the season is not finished:

(Q) = Qualified to the phase of tournament indicated; **(TQ)** = Qualified to tournament, but not yet to the particular phase indicated; **(DQ)** = Disqualified from tournament.

Head-to-Head: used when head-to-head record is used to rank tied teams.

Results summary

Overall								Home						Away					
Pld	W	D	L	GF	GA	GD	Pts	W	D	L	GF	GA	GD	W	D	L	GF	GA	GD
6	4	2	0	12	2	+10	14	3	0	0	10	1	+9	1	2	0	2	1	+1

Last updated: 3 October 2010

Source: Competitive Matches

Results by round

Round	01	02	03	04	05	06	07	08	09	10	11	12	13	14	15	16	17	18	19	20	21	22	23	24	25	26	27	28	29	30	31	32	33	34	35	36	37	38
Ground	A	H	A	H	A	H	A	H	A	H	A	H	A	H	A	H	A	H	A	H	A	H	A	H	A	H	A	H	A	H	A	H	A	H	A	H	A	H
Result	D	W	W	W	D	W																																
Position	10	5	3	1	4	3																																

Last updated: 3 October 2010.

Source: Competitive Matches

Ground: A = Away; H = Home. **Result**: D = Draw; L = Lose; W = Win; P = Postponed.

Champions League

Group G

Team	Pld	W	D	L	GF	GA	GD	Pts
Real Madrid	2	2	0	0	3	0	+3	**6**
Milan	2	1	1	0	3	1	+2	**4**
Ajax	2	0	1	1	1	3	−2	**1**
Auxerre	2	0	0	2	0	3	−3	**0**

	AJX	AUX	MIL	RM
Ajax	–	19 Oct	1–1	23 Nov
Auxerre	3 Nov	–	23 Nov	0–1
Milan	8 Dec	2–0	–	3 Nov
Real Madrid	2–0	8 Dec	19 Oct	–

Matches

Competitive

La Liga

M	Date	Tournament	Round	Ground	Opponent	Score[1]	Report
1	29 August 2010	La Liga	1	A	Mallorca	0 – 0	
2	11 September 2010	La Liga	2	H	Osasuna	1 – 0	
3	18 September 2010	La Liga	3	A	Real Sociedad	2 – 1	
4	21 September 2010	La Liga	4	H	Espanyol	3 – 0	
5	25 September 2010	La Liga	5	A	Levante	0 – 0	
6	3 October 2010	La Liga	6	H	Deportivo La Coruña	6 – 1	
7	16 October 2010	La Liga	7	A	Málaga		
8	24 October 2010	La Liga	8	H	Racing Santander		
9	31 October 2010	La Liga	9	A	Hércules		
10	7 November 2010	La Liga	10	H	Atlético Madrid		
11	14 November 2010	La Liga	11	A	Sporting de Gijón		
12	21 November 2010	La Liga	12	H	Athletic Bilbao		
13	28 November 2010	La Liga	13	A	Barcelona		
14	5 December 2010	La Liga	14	H	Valencia		
15	12 December 2010	La Liga	15	A	Zaragoza		
16	19 December 2010	La Liga	16	H	Sevilla		
17	2 January 2011	La Liga	17	A	Getafe		
18	9 January 2011	La Liga	18	H	Villarreal		
19	16 January 2011	La Liga	19	A	Almería		
20	23 January 2011	La Liga	20	H	Mallorca		
21	30 January 2011	La Liga	21	A	Osasuna		
22	6 February 2011	La Liga	22	H	Real Sociedad		
23	13 February 2011	La Liga	23	A	Espanyol		
24	20 February 2011	La Liga	24	H	Levante		
25	27 February 2011	La Liga	25	A	Deportivo La Coruña		
26	2 March 2011	La Liga	26	H	Málaga		

27	6 March 2011	La Liga	27	A	Racing Santander		
28	13 March 2011	La Liga	28	H	Hércules		
29	20 March 2011	La Liga	29	A	Atlético Madrid		
30	3 April 2011	La Liga	30	H	Sporting de Gijón		
31	10 April 2011	La Liga	31	A	Athletic Bilbao		
32	17 April 2011	La Liga	32	H	Barcelona		
33	24 April 2011	La Liga	33	A	Valencia		
34	1 May 2011	La Liga	34	H	Zaragoza		
35	8 May 2011	La Liga	35	A	Sevilla		
36	11 May 2011	La Liga	36	H	Getafe		
37	15 May 2011	La Liga	37	A	Villarreal		
38	22 May 2011	La Liga	38	H	Almería		

Last updated: 20 July 2010

Source: Realmadrid.com [37], LFP [38], La Liga Schedule [39], La Liga [40]

[1]Real Madrid goals come first.

National flags for *Ground* and *Opponent* columns are only shown when different to that of Real Madrid.

M = Match; Ground: **H** = Home, **A** = Away, **N** = Neutral, **HR** = Home replacement, **AR** = Away replacement.

UEFA Champions League

M	Date	Tournament	Round	Ground	Opponent	Score[1]	Report
1	15 September 2010	UEFA Champions League	Group stage	H	Ajax	2 – 0	
2	28 September 2010	UEFA Champions League	Group stage	A	Auxerre	1 – 0	
3	19 October 2010	UEFA Champions League	Group stage	H	Milan		
4	3 November 2010	UEFA Champions League	Group stage	A	Milan		
5	23 November 2010	UEFA Champions League	Group stage	A	Ajax		
6	8 December 2010	UEFA Champions League	Group stage	H	Auxerre		

Last updated: 30 August 2010

Source: Realmadrid.com [41], Draws [42], Group stage Matches [43]

[1]Real Madrid goals come first.

National flags for *Ground* and *Opponent* columns are only shown when different to that of Real Madrid.

M = Match; Ground: **H** = Home, **A** = Away, **N** = Neutral, **HR** = Home replacement, **AR** = Away replacement.

Copa Del Rey

M	Date	Tournament	Round	Ground	Opponent	Score[1]	Report
1	27 October 2010	Copa del Rey	Round of 32 (1st leg)	A	Murcia		
2	10 November 2010	Copa del Rey	Round of 32 (2nd leg)	H	Murcia		

Last updated: 22 September 2010

Source: Sorteo deciseisavos Copa del Rey [44]

[1]Real Madrid goals come first.

National flags for *Ground* and *Opponent* columns are only shown when different to that of Real Madrid.

M = Match; Ground: **H** = Home, **A** = Away, **N** = Neutral, **HR** = Home replacement, **AR** = Away replacement.

Pre-season and friendlies

M	Date	Tournament	Round	Ground	Opponent	Score[1]	Report
1	4 August 2010	US Tour	–	N	América	3 – 2	
2	7 August 2010	US Tour	–	N	LA Galaxy	3 – 2	
3	13 August 2010	Franz Beckenbauer Testimonial	–	A	Bayern Munich	0 – 0 (4–2 pen.)	
4	17 August 2010	European Tour	–	A	Standard	1 – 1	
5	22 August 2010	Ciudad de Alicante Trophy	–	A	Hércules	3 – 1	
6	24 August 2010	Santiago Bernabéu Trophy	–	H	Peñarol	2 – 0	

Last updated: 11 June 2010

Source: Preseason [45], US Tour [46], US & European Tour [47], Santiago Bernabéu Trophy [48]

[1]Real Madrid goals come first.

Country's flag depict country of foreign team to that of Real Madrid.

Ground: H = Home; A = Away; N = Neutral; **HR** = Home replacement; **AR** = Away replacement; **GD** = Goal difference

See also

- 2010–11 Copa del Rey
- 2010–11 La Liga
- 2010–11 UEFA Champions League

External links

- Official website [6]
- Real Madrid Team Page [49]
- Real Madrid (Spain) profile [50]

List of Real Madrid C.F. players

Raúl González has made more than 700 appearances for Real Madrid. He is the all-time top scorer of the club, with 323 goals.

Real Madrid C.F. is a professional association football club based in Madrid, Spain, that plays in La Liga. The club was formed in 1902 as Madrid Football Club, and played its first competitive match on 19 May 1902, when it entered the semi-final of the Campeonato de Copa de S.M. Alfonso XIII. Real Madrid was one of the founding members of La Liga in 1929, and is one of three clubs, including FC Barcelona and Athletic Bilbao, to have never been relegated from the league. Since then, the club's first team has competed in numerous nationally and internationally organised competitions. Real is the most successful club in Spanish football along with FC Barcelona, having won a total of 58 domestic titles; a record 31 La Liga titles, 17 Spanish Cups, eight Spanish Super Cups, one Copa Eva Duarte and one League Cup. Real is one of the most successful clubs in European football, having won twelve official UEFA trophies in total.

Raúl holds the record for most overall appearances, having played 741 from 1994 to 2010, ahead of Manuel Sanchís, Jr, who has made 711 appearances from 1983 to 2001. Santillana is third with 643 appearances for the club. Raúl has scored the most goals with 323, of which 228 were scored in league competition, making him the Real Madrid player who has scored the most goals in the league. Alfredo Di Stefano is second with 307 goals, and Santillana is third, having scored 290 goals. Ferenc Puskás holds the record for the most goals in a season; he scored 48 goals in competitions during the 1959–60 season. Hugo Sánchez holds the record for league goals scored in a season, having scored 38 goals in La Liga in 1989–90.

Real Madrid has employed several famous players, with four FIFA World Player and six Ballon d'Or winners among the previous and current club players.

The list includes notable footballers who have played for Real Madrid. Generally, this means players that have played at least 100 matches for the club. However, some players who have played fewer matches are also included if they are recognized as official club legends by Real Madrid.

Key

†	Club captains who have won a major senior competition
*	Club record holder
¤	Played their full career at Real Madrid

- Players whose name is in *italics* currently play for the club.
- The years are the first and last calendar years in which the player appeared in competitive first-team football for the club.
- The total appearances and goals comprise those in La Liga, Copa del Rey, Supercopa de España, UEFA Champions League, UEFA Cup, UEFA Super Cup, FIFA Club World Cup and several now-defunct competitions, including the Copa Eva Duarte, Copa de la Liga, Latin Cup, Copa Iberoamericana, Campeonato Centro, Intercontinental Cup and UEFA Cup Winners' Cup.

List of players

Statistics correct as of match played on 21 September 2010.

do Di Stéfano became the
Real Madrid player to win
ie Ballon d'Or in 1957.

Hugo Sánchez is the record goalscorer in a league season for Real, with 38, and the second all-time goalscorer in La Liga.

selections, Iker made the most al appearances as a Madrid player.

Name	Nationality	Position[NB]	Real Madrid career	Captaincy	Appearances	Goals	Notes
Félix Quesada	Spain	Defender	1922–1936	—	244	33	
Jose María Peña	Spain	Midfielder	1926–1932	—	147	6	
Jaime Lazcano	Spain	Midfielder	1928–1935	—	115	62	
Ricardo Zamora*	Spain	Goalkeeper	1930–1936	—	112	0	[A]
Eugenio Hilario	Spain	Forward	1930–1936	—	105	28	
Nervin Nepomuceno	Spain	Forward	1931–1936	—	121	42	
Jacinto Quincoces	Spain	Defender	1931–1941	—	167	0	
Leoncito	Spain	Midfielder	1931–1942	—	149	9	
Pedro Regueiro	Spain	Midfielder	1932–1936	—	104	0	
José Ramón Sauto	Mexico	Midfielder	1934–1936	—	124	0	
Simón Lecue	Spain	Forward	1935–1942	—	118	39	

Juan Antonio Ipiña	Spain	Midfielder	1936–1949	—	293	11	
Chus Alonso	Spain	Midfielder	1939–1948	—	160	65	
Sabino Barinaga	Spain	Midfielder	1940–1950	—	185	93	
Antonio Alsúa	Spain	Forward	1941–1948	—	176	45	
Félix Huete	Spain	Midfielder	1941–1948	—	181	1	
Clemente	Spain	Defender	1941–1952	—	144	0	
Corona	Spain	Defender	1942–1948	—	153	9	
Moleiro	Spain	Midfielder	1942–1948	—	107	10	
Pruden	Spain	Forward	1943–1948	—	114	93	
José Bañón Gonzálvez	Spain	Goalkeeper	1943–1949	—	159	0	
Luis Molowny	Spain	Forward	1946–1957	—	171	89	
Pablo Olmedo	Spain	Midfielder	1948–1953	—	108	36	
Pahiño	Spain	Forward	1948–1953	—	124	108	[Pichichi]
Miguel Muñoz	Spain	Midfielder	1948–1958	1948–1958†	347	23	
Joaquín Navarro	Spain	Defender	1949–1957	—	213	2	
Juanito Alonso	Spain	Goalkeeper	1949–1961	—	297	0	
Joaquín Oliva	Spain	Defender	1950–1957	—	119	0	
Roque Olsen	Argentina	Forward	1950–1957	—	123	66	
Joseíto	Spain	Forward	1951–1959	—	164	70	
José María Zárraga	Spain	Midfielder	1951–1962	1958–1961†	306	96	
Rafael Lesmes	Spain	Defender	1952–1960	—	218	1	
Alfredo Di Stéfano*	Argentina/ Spain	Forward	1953–1964	—	396	307	[d'Or][Pichichi][B]
Francisco Gento	Spain	Forward	1953–1971	1961–1971†	605	183	
Héctor Rial	Spain/ Argentina	Midfielder	1954–1961	—	165	81	
Marquitos	Spain	Defender	1954–1962	—	159	2	
Juan Santisteban	Spain	Midfielder	1955–1960, 1962–1965	—	114	4	
Raymond Kopa	France	Forward	1956–1959	—	101	31	[d'Or]

Casado Bucho	Spain	Defender	1956–1966	—	125	1	
José Santamaría	Spain/ Uruguay	Defender	1957–1966	—	226	2	
Ferenc Puskás*	Hungary/ Spain	Forward	1958–1966	—	263	240	[Pichichi][C]
Pachín	Spain	Forward	1959–1968	—	164	2	
Manuel Bueno	Spain	Midfielder	1959–1971	—	118	27	
José Vicente Train*	Spain	Goalkeeper	1960–1964	—	100	0	[A]
Antonio Betancort	Spain	Goalkeeper	1961–1962, 1963–1971	—	177	0	
Isidro Sánchez	Spain	Defender	1961–1965	—	103	1	
Félix Ruiz	Spain	Midfielder	1961–1968	—	145	44	
Vicente Miera	Spain	Defender	1961–1969	—	125	1	
Ignacio Zoco	Spain	Midfielder	1962–1974	1971–1974†	318	8	
Amancio	Spain	Forward	1962–1976	1974–1976†	471	155	[Pichichi]
Antonio Calpe Hernández	Spain	Defender	1963–1971	—	122	3	
Pedro de Felipe	Spain	Defender	1963–1972	—	167	0	
Manuel Sanchís, Sr	Spain	Defender	1964–1971	—	143	1	
José Luis	Spain	Defender	1964–1976	—	182	16	
Ramón Moreno Grosso	Spain	Forward	1964–1976	—	366	75	
Pirri	Spain	Midfielder	1964–1979	1976–1979†	595	210	
Manuel Velázquez	Spain	Midfielder	1965–1977	—	345	53	
Fernando Zunzunegui Rodríguez	Spain	Defender	1966–1972	—	110	5	
José Antonio Grande	Spain	Defender	1968–1973	—	121	14	
Miguel Ángel	Spain	Goalkeeper	1968–1985	—	445	0	
Gregorio Benito	Spain	Defender	1969–1982	—	420	2	
Juan Carlos Touriño	Argentina	Defender	1970–1976	—	123	0	

Javier Aguilar	Spain	Forward	1971–1979	—	190	50	
Mariano García Remón	Spain	Goalkeeper	1971–1984	—	231	0	
Santillana*	Spain	Forward	1971–1988	1979–1988†	643	290	[D]
Vicente del Bosque	Spain	Midfielder	1973–1984	—	342	25	
Antonio Camacho	Spain	Defender	1973–1989¤	—	577	11	
Günter Netzer	Germany	Midfielder	1974–1976	—	100	13	
Paul Breitner	Germany	Midfielder	1974–1977	—	101	10	
Juan Roberto Martínez Martínez	Spain/ Argentina	Forward	1974–1980	—	169	52	
Juan Cruz Sol	Spain	Defender	1975–1979	—	125	0	
Henning Jensen	Denmark	Forward	1976–1979	—	102	18	
Isidoro San José	Spain	Midfielder	1976–1986	—	225	6	
Andrés Sabido	Spain	Defender	1977–1982	—	117	3	
Isidro	Spain	Forward	1977–1985	—	232	22	
Ulrich Stielike	Germany	Midfielder	1977–1985	—	310	51	
Juanito	Spain	Forward	1977–1987	—	401	121	[Pichichi]
Francisco García Hernández	Spain	Midfielder	1978–1983	—	129	36	
Ángel de los Santos Cano	Spain	Midfielder	1979–1985	—	237	13	
Francisco Pineda	Spain	Forward	1980–1985	—	145	43	
Ricardo Gallego	Spain	Midfielder	1980–1989	—	372	28	
Agustín	Spain	Goalkeeper	1980–1990	—	125	0	
Antonio Salguero	Spain	Defender	1981–1987	—	138	8	
Míchel	Spain	Midfielder	1981–1996	—	404	97	
Chendo	Spain	Defender	1982–1998¤	—	497	3	
Rafael Martín Vázquez	Spain	Midfielder	1983–1990	—	179	35	
Emilio Butragueño	Spain	Forward	1983–1995	—	463	170	[Pichichi]
Manuel Sanchís, Jr	Spain	Defender	1983–2001¤	1988–2001†	711	41	

Jorge Valdano	Argentina	Forward	1984–1987	—	120	56	
Jesús Solana	Spain	Defender	1985–1991	—	149	2	
Hugo Sánchez*	Mexico	Forward	1985–1992	—	207	164	[Pichichi][E]
Rafael Gordillo	Spain	Midfielder	1985–1992	—	254	27	
Paco Buyo	Spain	Goalkeeper	1986–1997	—	454	0	
Miguel Tendillo	Spain	Defender	1987–1992	—	145	12	
Francisco Llorente Gento	Spain	Forward	1987–1994	—	160	11	
Fernando Hierro	Spain	Defender	1989–2003	2001–2003†	598	126	
Alfonso Pérez	Spain	Forward	1990–1995	—	121	21	
Luis Enrique	Spain	Midfielder	1991–1996	—	175	17	
Mikel Lasa	Spain	Defender	1991–1997	—	178	5	
Iván Zamorano	Chile	Forward	1992–1996	—	173	100	[Pichichi]
Rafael Alkorta	Spain	Defender	1993–1997	—	135	3	
Emilio Amavisca	Spain	Midfielder	1994–1996	—	144	15	
Fernando Redondo	Argentina	Midfielder	1994–2000	—	228	5	
Raúl*	Spain	Forward	1994–2010	2003–2010†	741	323	[Pichichi][F]
Guti	Spain	Midfielder	1995–2010	—	542	77	
Predrag Mijatović	Montenegro	Forward	1996–1999	—	118	37	
Bodo Illgner	Germany	Goalkeeper	1996–2001	—	120	0	
Davor Šuker	Croatia	Forward	1996–1999	—	106	38	
Roberto Carlos	Brazil	Defender	1996–2007	—	527	69	
Sávio	Brazil	Forward	1997–2000	—	160	31	
Aitor Karanka	Spain	Defender	1997–2002	—	149	0	
Fernando Morientes	Spain	Forward	1997–2005	—	270	100	
Steve McManaman	England	Forward	1999–2003	—	157	14	
Iván Helguera	Spain	Defender	1999–2007	—	346	33	
Míchel Salgado	Spain	Defender	1999–2009	—	371	5	
*Iker Casillas**	Spain	Goalkeeper	1999–¤	2010–	523	0	[G]

Claude Makélélé	France/ Zaire	Midfielder	2000–2003	—	143	1	
Albert Celades	Spain	Midfielder	2000–2005	—	100	5	
Santiago Solari	Argentina	Midfielder	2000–2005	—	209	22	
Luís Figo*	Portugal	Forward	2000–2005	—	244	57	|FIFA||d'Or||H|
Zinedine Zidane	France	Midfielder	2001–2006	—	227	49	|FIFA|
Raúl Bravo	Spain	Defender	2001–2007	—	133	4	
Francisco Pavón	Spain	Defender	2001–2007	—	128	2	
Ronaldo*	Brazil	Forward	2002–2007	—	177	104	|FIFA||d'Or||Pichichi||I|
David Beckham	England	Midfielder	2003–2007	—	159	20	
Robinho	Brazil	Forward	2005–2008	—	137	35	
Sergio Ramos	Spain	Defender	2005–	—	219	28	
Fabio Cannavaro	Italy	Defender	2006–2009	—	117	2	|FIFA||d'Or|
Gonzalo Higuaín	Argentina/ France	Forward	2006–	—	146	66	
Mahamadou Diarra	Mali	Midfielder	2006–	—	117	4	
Fernando Gago	Argentina	Midfielder	2007–	—	114	1	
Marcelo	Brazil	Defender	2007–	—	120	8	

|- |align="left"|*Mesut Özil*||*align=left*| *Turkey*||*Midfielder*||*2010–20..*||—|||||[*FIFA*]

Notes

For a full description of positions see football positions.

- d'Or. [a] [b] [c] [d] [e] Won Ballon d'Or while at Real Madrid.
- FIFA. [a] [b] [c] [d] Won FIFA Player of the Year while at Real Madrid.
- Pichichi.[a] [b] [c] [d] [e] [f] [g] [h] [i] [j] Won the Pichichi Trophy while at Real Madrid.
- A. Zamora has Real's record of Zamora trophies, with three trophies won (record shared with José Vicente Train).
- B. Di Stéfano was the first Real Madrid player to win the Ballon d'Or in 1957.
- C. Puskás is record goalscorer in one match, with six goals (record shared with Benguría).
- D

References

- "Legends" [1]. Real Madrid C.F. Retrieved 10 September 2008.
- "Database - Real Madrid football players 1902-2009" [2] (in Spanish). leyendablanca. Retrieved 2009-09-09.
- "Database - Players" [3] (in Hungarian). madridista.hu. Retrieved 10 September 2009.

Specific

List of Real Madrid C.F. managers

Real Madrid C.F. is a professional association football club based in Madrid, Spain, which plays in La Liga. This chronological list comprises all those who have held the position of manager of the first team of Real Madrid from 1910, when the first professional manager was appointed, to the present day. Each manager's entry includes his dates of tenure and the club's overall competitive record (in terms of matches won, drawn and lost), honours won and significant achievements while under his care. Caretaker managers are included, where known. As of the start of the 2008–09 season, Real Madrid have had 32 full-time managers.

The first full-time manager for Real Madrid was Arthur Johnson. He was signed by one of the founders of Real Madrid, and then director, Adolfo Meléndez, and coached the team for ten seasons, gaining four Spanish Cups.

The most successful Real Madrid manager in terms of trophies won is Miguel Muñoz, who won nine La Liga titles, two Copa del Rey trophies, two UEFA Champions League titles and one Intercontinental Cup in his 15-year reign as manager. He is also the club's longest-serving manager. Chilean Manuel Pellegrini is Real's most successful permanent manager in terms of winning percentage with 75%, while José Quirante is team's least successful (38.89%).

Key

- **GF** = Goals for
- **GA** = Goals against
- **Win%** = Percentage of win

List of managers

Information correct as of 21 September 2010. Only competitive matches are counted.

Name	Nationality	From	To	Matches[A]	Won	Drawn	Lost	GF	GA	Win%[B]	Honours	Notes
Arthur Johnson	England	1910	1920	23	11	3	9	48	39	47.83	5 Copa del Rey	[C][D]
Juan de Cárcer	Spain	1920	1926	22	10	2	10	38	45	45.45		[C]
Pedro Llorente	Spain	1926	1926	0	0	0	0	0	0	—		[C]
Santiago Bernabéu Yeste	Spain	1926	1927	8	5	0	3	31	15	62.50		[C]
José Berraondo	Spain	1927	1929	41	27	4	10	115	58	65.85		[C]
José Quirante	Spain	1929	1930	18	7	3	8	45	42	38.89		[C]
Lippo Hertzka	Hungary	1930	1932	52	26	15	11	95	58	50.00	1 La Liga	
Robert Firth	England	1932	1934	45	30	5	10	126	52	66.67	1 La Liga	
Francisco Bru	Spain	1934	1941	118	71	13	34	290	152	60.17	2 Copa del Rey	
Juan Armet	Spain	1941	September 1943	46	23	7	16	96	72	50.00		
Ramón Encinas	Spain	September 1943	May 1945	84	45	15	24	199	126	53.57		
Jacinto Quincoces	Spain	May 1945	March 1946	35	18	10	7	70	37	51.43	1 Copa del Rey	[C]
Baltasar Albéniz	Spain	March 1946	April 1947	35	18	5	12	82	66	51.43		
Jacinto Quincoces	Spain	April 1947	January 1948	17	5	4	8	32	41	29.41		
Michael Keeping	England	January 1948	October 1950	82	37	20	25	192	153	45.12		
Baltasar Albéniz	Spain	October 1950	March 1951	16	7	2	7	41	37	43.75	1 Copa del Rey	
Héctor Scarone	Uruguay	March 1951	April 1952	48	25	10	13	113	73	52.08		

Juan Antonio Ipiña	Spain	April 1952	May 1953	34	21	2	11	82	57	61.76		[C]
Enrique Fernández	Uruguay	May 1953	December 1954	50	31	8	11	126	60	62.00	1 La Liga	
José Villalonga	Spain	December 1954	April 1957	105	66	14	25	269	141	62.86	2 La Liga 2 European Cup	[E]
Luis Carniglia	Argentina	April 1957	February 1959	68	48	11	9	178	58	70.59	1 La Liga 1 European Cup	
Miguel Muñoz	Spain	February 1959	April 1959	9	5	2	2	31	9	55.56		[C]
Luis Carniglia	Argentina	April 1959	July 1959	13	8	1	4	28	16	61.54	1 European Cup	
Manuel Fleitas	Paraguay	July 1959	April 1960	33	23	4	6	109	42	69.70		
Miguel Muñoz	Spain	April 1960	January 1974	595	352	126	117	1194	553	59.16	9 La Liga 2 Copa del Rey 2 European Cup 1 Intercontinental Cup	
Luis Molowny	Spain	January 1974	May 1974	23	13	2	8	49	26	56.52	1 Copa del Rey	[C]
Miljan Miljanić	Yugoslavia	May 1974	September 1977	134	67	36	31	231	150	50.00	2 La Liga 1 Copa del Rey	
Luis Molowny	Spain	September 1977	June 1979	90	51	24	15	196	94	56.67	2 La Liga	
Vujadin Boškov	Yugoslavia	June 1979	March 1982	139	80	31	28	249	136	57.55	1 La Liga 1 Copa del Rey	
Luis Molowny	Spain	March 1982	April 1982	6	4	1	1	11	7	66.67	1 Copa del Rey	
Alfredo di Stéfano	Argentina	April 1982	April 1984	108	63	23	22	192	113	58.33		[C]

Amancio Amaro	Spain	April 1984	April 1985	47	19	13	15	69	52	40.43		[C]
Luis Molowny	Spain	April 1985	April 1986	61	39	7	15	137	67	63.93	1 La Liga 2 UEFA Cup 1 Copa de la Liga	
Leo Beenhakker	Netherlands	April 1986	June 1989	169	107	40	22	357	158	63.31	3 La Liga 1 Copa del Rey 1 Supercopa de España	
John Toshack	Wales	June 1989	November 1990	64	41	15	8	161	56	64.06	1 La Liga 1 Supercopa de España	
Alfredo di Stéfano	Argentina	November 1990	March 1991	21	9	3	9	32	22	42.86	1 Supercopa de España	
Radomir Antić	Yugoslavia	March 1991	January 1992	39	27	6	6	84	32	69.23		
Leo Beenhakker	Netherlands	January 1992	June 1992	28	14	7	7	47	27	50.00		
Benito Floro	Spain	June 1992	March 1994	92	52	21	19	165	90	56.52	1 Copa del Rey 1 Supercopa de España	
Vicente del Bosque	Spain	March 1994	May 1994	11	5	1	5	23	22	45.45	1 Supercopa de España	[C]
Jorge Valdano	Argentina	May 1994	January 1996	78	39	17	22	142	87	50.00	1 La Liga	[C]
Vicente del Bosque	Spain	January 1996	January 1996	1	1	0	0	5	0	100.00		
Arsenio Iglesias	Spain	January 1996	May 1996	21	11	4	6	33	22	52.38		
Fabio Capello	Italy	May 1996	June 1997	48	31	12	5	96	41	64.58	1 La Liga	
Jupp Heynckes	Germany	June 1997	May 1998	53	26	15	12	92	55	49.06	1 Supercopa de España 1 UEFA Champions League	

Guus Hiddink	Netherlands	May 1998	February 1999	34	19	4	11	73	48	55.88	1 Intercontinental Cup	
John Toshack	Wales	February 1999	November 1999	37	19	9	9	73	62	51.35		
Vicente del Bosque	Spain	November 1999	23 June 2003	233	127	56	50	461	267	54.51	2 La Liga 2 UEFA Champions League 2 Supercopa de España 1 UEFA Super Cup 1 Intercontinental Cup	
Carlos Queiroz	Portugal	25 June 2003	31 May 2004	59	34	11	14	113	76	57.63	1 Supercopa de España	
José Antonio Camacho	Spain	1 June 2004	1 July 2004	6	4	0	2	7	5	66.67		[C]
Mariano García Remón	Spain	1 July 2004	30 December 2004	20	12	4	4	37	18	60.00		[C]
Vanderlei Luxemburgo	Brazil	30 December 2004	3 December 2005	45	28	7	10	83	45	62.22		
Juan Ramón López Caro	Spain	3 December 2005	5 July 2006	48	23	13	12	82	50	47.92		
Fabio Capello	Italy	5 July 2006	28 June 2007	50	28	12	10	91	55	56.00	1 La Liga	
Bernd Schuster	Germany	9 July 2007	9 December 2008	75	44	9	22	156	100	58.67	1 La Liga 1 Supercopa de España	[C]
Juande Ramos	Spain	9 December 2008	30 June 2009	27	18	1	8	53	34	66.67		
Manuel Pellegrini	Chile	1 July 2009	26 May 2010	48	36	5	7	119	48	75.00		

José Mourinho	Portugal	28 May 2010	*present*	7	5	2	0	8	1	71.43		

Notes

A. ^ Campeonato Centro matches are not counted because it was a regional championship

B. ^ Win% is rounded to two decimal places

C. a b c d e f g h i j k l m n o p q Formerly played for the club

D. Club's first full-time manager

E. The first manager to manage a Spanish club side in European competition and to win a European trophy (1960 European Cup)

References

- Coaches [1] on Real Madrid official site

Specific

List of Real Madrid C.F. presidents

Real Madrid C.F. is a football club based in Madrid, Spain that competes in La Liga, the most senior football league in Spain. Since its founding in 1902, the club has had 19 different presidents. The club is owned by the club-members of Real Madrid C.F., and similarly to a limited liability company, they elect the president by a ballot. The president has the responsibility for the overall management of the club, including formally signing contracts with players and staff. In Spain, it is customary for the president to watch the games in which the first-team participates, together with the president from the opposing team.

Since its foundation, Real Madrid C.F. has been owned and operated only by its members (all Spanish) called *socios*, unlike most European football clubs. Santiago Bernabéu Yeste remains the longest-running president of The Whites (35 years, from 1943 to 1978). In addition, under Bernabéu's presidency the club won the most trophies (28). On July 2000, former Real player Alfredo Di Stéfano was appointed Honourary President of the Club.

List of presidents

As of 1 June 2009.

Florentino Pérez is the current president of the club and the only one who presidented Real twice.

Name	From	To
Julián Palacios	1900	6 March 1902
Juan Padrós	6 March 1902	January 1904
Carlos Padrós	January 1904	1908
Adolfo Meléndez	1908	July 1916
Pedro Parages	July 1916	16 May 1926
Luis de Urquijo	16 May 1926	1930
Luis Usera	1930	31 May 1935
Rafael Sánchez Guerra	31 May 1935	4 August 1936
Adolfo Meléndez	4 August 1936	1940
Antonio Santos Peralba	1940	11 September 1943
Santiago Bernabéu Yeste	11 September 1943	2 June 1978
Luis de Carlos	September 1978	24 May 1985
Ramón Mendoza	24 May 1985	26 November 1995
Lorenzo Sanz	26 November 1995	16 July 2000
Florentino Pérez	16 July 2000	27 February 2006
Fernando Martín Álvarez	27 February 2006	26 April 2006
Luis Gómez-Montejano	26 April 2006	2 July 2006
Ramón Calderón	2 July 2006	16 January 2009

Vicente Boluda	16 January 2009	31 May 2009
Florentino Pérez	1 June 2009	*present*

List of Real Madrid C.F. records and statistics

Real Madrid C.F. is a Spanish professional association football club based in Madrid. The club was formed in 1902 as *Madrid Football Club*, and played its first competitive match on May 19, 1902, when it entered the semi-final of the Campeonato de Copa de S.M. Alfonso XIII. Real Madrid currently plays in La Liga, the top tier of Spanish football. Madrid was one of the founding members of La Liga in 1929, and is one of three clubs, including FC Barcelona and Athletic Bilbao, never to have been relegated from the league. They have also been involved in European football ever since they became the first Spanish club to enter the European Cup in 1955, excepting 1977-78 and 1996-97 seasons. From the statistics, Real Madrid are the best team of the 2010 season.

Raúl González is the all-time top goalscorer and the record appearances maker of the club.

This list encompasses the major honours won by Real Madrid and records set by the club, their managers and their players. The player records section includes details of the club's leading goalscorers and those who have made most appearances in first-team competitions. It also records notable achievements by Real Madrid players on the international stage, and the highest transfer fees paid and received by the club.

The club currently holds the record for the most European Cup/UEFA Champions League triumphs with 9, and the most La Liga titles with 31. The club's record appearance maker was Raúl, who had made 741 appearances from 1994 to 2010; the club's record goalscorer is also Raúl, who scored 323 goals in all competitions during his career.

All stats accurate as of 6 August 2010.

Honours

Historically, Real Madrid is Spain's most successful team, having won 58 domestic trophies, and one of the most recognized football clubs in the world, having won 15 international trophies, making them the second most successful team in Europe and third in the world for official international competition won, all recognized by UEFA and FIFA; it also has the record in La Liga titles (with 31), Supercopa de España titles (with 8) and European Cup/UEFA Champions League titles (with 9). The club was placed first in the FIFA Clubs of the 20th Century's selection on 23 December 2000. It also received the FIFA Order of Merit in 2004. Added to this, Real is allowed to wear a multiple-winner badge on their shirt during UEFA Champions League matches as they have won more than five European Cups.

Regional Competitions

- **Trofeos Mancomunados: 23** (record)
  - 1904-05, 1905-06, 1906-07, 1907-08, 1909-10, 1912-13, 1915-16, 1916-17, 1917-18, 1919-20, 1921-22, 1922-23, 1923-24, 1925-26, 1926-27, 1928-29, 1929-30, 1930-31, 1931-32, 1932-33, 1933-34, 1934-35, 1935-36.

Domestic Competitions

League

- **La Liga: 31** (record)
  - 1931–32, 1932–33, 1953–54, 1954–55, 1956–57, 1957–58, 1960–61, 1961–62, 1962–63, 1963–64, 1964–65, 1966–67, 1967–68, 1968–69, 1971–72, 1974–75, 1975–76, 1977–78, 1978–79, 1979–80, 1985–86, 1986–87, 1987–88, 1988–89, 1989–90, 1994–95, 1996–97, 2000–01, 2002–03, 2006–07, 2007–08

Cup

- **Copa del Rey: 17**
  - 1905, 1906, 1907, 1908, 1917, 1933–34, 1935–36, 1945–46, 1946–47, 1961–62, 1969–70, 1973–74, 1974–75, 1979–80, 1981–82, 1988–89, 1992–93
- **Supercopa de España: 8**
  - 1988, 1989*, 1990, 1993, 1997, 2001, 2003, 2008

    (Won Copa del Rey and La Liga)*
- **Copa Eva Duarte: 1**
  - 1947
- **Copa de la Liga: 1**
  - 1985

European Competitions

Official Titles

- **European Cup/ UEFA Champions League: 9** (record)
  - 1955–56*, 1956–57, 1957–58, 1958–59, 1959–60, 1965–66, 1997–98, 1999–2000, 2001–02

    (* *First ever winners*)
- **UEFA Cup/ UEFA Europa League: 2**
  - 1984–85, 1985–86
- **UEFA European Super Cup: 1**
  - 2002

Unofficial Titles

- **Latin Cup: 2**
  - 1955, 1957
- **Copa Iberoamericana: 1**
  - 1994

Worldwide Competitions

- **Intercontinental Cup/ FIFA Club World Cup: 3** (record)
  - 1960, 1998, 2002

Friendly Competitions

Created by Real Madrid

- **Santiago Bernabeu Trophy: 21** (record)
  - 1981, 1983, 1984, 1985, 1987, 1989, 1991, 1994, 1995, 1996, 1997, 1998, 1999, 2000, 2003, 2005, 2006, 2007, 2008, 2009, 2010

Created by other clubs

- **Trofeos Teresa Herrera: 8**
  - 1949, 1953, 1966, 1976, 1978, 1979, 1980, 1994
- **Trofeos Ramón de Carranza: 6**
  - 1958, 1959, 1960, 1966, 1970, 1982
- **Trofeos Ciudad de La Línea: 5**
  - 1978, 1981, 1982, 1986, 2000
- **Trofeos Ciutat de Palma: 4**

  - 1975, 1980, 1983, 1990
- **Trofeos Ciudad de Barcelona: 3**
  - 1983, 1985, 1988
- **Trofeos Euskadi Asegarce: 3**
  - 1994, 1995, 1996
- **Trofeos Colombino: 3**
  - 1970, 1984, 1989
- **Pequeña Copa del Mundo de Clubes: 2**
  - 1952, 1956
- **Trofeos Naranja: 2**
  - 1990, 2003
- **Trofeos Costa del Sol: 2**
  - 1970, 1976
- **Trofeos Ciudad de Vigo: 2**
  - 1981, 1982
- **Trofeo Centenario AC Milan: 1**
  - 2000
- **Trofeo Benito Villamarín: 1**
  - 1960
- **Trofeo Mohamed V: 1**
  - 1966
- **Trofeo Ciudad de Caracas: 1**
  - 1980
- **Trofeo Año Santo Compostelano: 1**
  - 1970
- **Trofeo Jesús Gil: 1**
  - 2005
- **Taci Oil Cup: 1**
  - 2009
- **Franz Beckenbauer Testimonial: 1**
  - 2010

Players

See also: List of Real Madrid C.F. players

Appearances

- Youngest first-team player: Alberto Rivera, 17 years, 114 days (against Celta Vigo, La Liga, 10 June 1995)
- Oldest first-team player: -
- Oldest post-Second World War player: -
- Most consecutive League appearances: -
- Shortest appearance: -

Most appearances

Competitive, professional matches only.

	Name	Years	League	Cup	Europe	Other[A]	Total
1	Raúl	1994–2010	550	37	135	19	**741**
2	Manuel Sanchís	1983–2001	524	67	99	21	**711**
3	Carlos Santillana	1971–1988	461	84	87	11	**643**
4	Francisco Gento	1953–1971	428	75	96	6	**605**
5	Fernando Hierro	1989–2003	439	40	101	18	**598**
6	José Camacho	1973–1989	414	61	90	12	**577**
7	Pirri	1964–1979	417	67	75	2	**561**
8	Míchel	1981–1996	404	53	89	14	**560**
9	Guti	1995–2010	386	40	101	14	**541**
10	Roberto Carlos	1996–2007	370	33	109	15	**527**

Goalscorers

- Most goals in a season in all competitions: **48** - Ferenc Puskás, 1959–60
- Most League goals in a season: **38** - Hugo Sánchez, 1989–90
- Top League scorer with fewest goals in a season: **14** - Amancio Amaro, 1968–69
- Most goals scored in a league match: **5**
  - Manuel Alday v Espanyol, 28 February 1943
  - Antonio Alsúa v Castellón, 2 February 1947
  - Miguel Muñoz v Lleida, 30 January 1951

  - Pepillo v Elche, 7 February 1960
  - Ferenc Puskás v Elche, 22 January 1961
  - Fernando Morientes v Las Palmas, 9 February 2002
- Most goals scored in a Copa del Rey match: **6**
  - Benguría v Extremeño, 6 March 1927
  - Ferenc Puskás v Real Betis, 18 June 1961
- Youngest goalscorer – Alberto Rivera, 17 years, 114 days v Celta Vigo, La Liga, 10 June 1995
- Fastest goal: **14 seconds** - Ronaldo v Atlético Madrid, La Liga, 3 December 2003
- Fastest hat-trick: -
- Fastest four goals: -
- Most hat-tricks: -

Overall scorers

Competitive, professional matches only, appearances including substitutes appear in brackets.

	Name	Years	League	Cup	Europe	Other[A]	Total
1	Raúl	1994–2010	228 (550)	18 (37)	66 (135)	11 (19)	**323** (741)
2	/ Alfredo di Stéfano	1953–1964	216 (282)	39 (50)	49 (58)	3 (6)	**307** (396)
3	Carlos Santillana	1971–1988	186 (461)	48 (84)	47 (87)	9 (11)	**290** (643)
4	/ Ferenc Puskás	1958–1966	156 (182)	47 (41)	35 (38)	2 (2)	**240** (263)
5	Hugo Sánchez	1985–1992	164 (207)	19 (37)	23 (39)	2 (4)	**209** (287)
6	Francisco Gento	1952–1970	126 (428)	20 (75)	31 (96)	4 (6)	**183** (605)
7	Pirri	1964–1979	123 (417)	26 (67)	22 (75)	0 (2)	**171** (561)
8	Emilio Butragueño	1983–1995	122 (341)	16 (39)	25 (75)	7 (8)	**170** (463)
9	Amancio Amaro	1962–1976	119 (344)	14 (58)	22 (67)	0 (2)	**155** (471)
10	Míchel González	1981–1996	97 (404)	9 (53)	18 (89)	6 (14)	**130** (560)

Historical goals

Goal	Name	Date	Match
1st ever	Arthur Johnson	13 May 1902	Barcelona 3 - Real Madrid 1
1st in La Liga	Jaime Lazcano	10 February 1929	Real Madrid 5 - Europa 0
1000th	Pahiño	5 November 1950	Athletic 2 - Real Madrid 5
2000th	Francisco Gento	9 November 1963	Real Madrid 3 - Pontevedra 1
3000th	Juanito	20 January 1982	Salamanca 1 - Real Madrid 3
4000th	Iván Zamorano	22 December 1994	Valladolid 0 - Real Madrid 5
5000th	Guti	14 September 2008	Real Madrid 4 - Numancia 3

Award winners

Ballon d'Or

The following players have won the Ballon d'Or while playing for Real Madrid:

- Alfredo di Stéfano – 1957, 1959
- Raymond Kopa – 1958
- Luís Figo – 2000
- Ronaldo – 2002
- Fabio Cannavaro – 2006

European Golden Shoe

The following players have won the European Golden Shoe while playing for Real Madrid:

- Hugo Sánchez (38 goals) – 1990

UEFA Club Footballer of the Year

The following players have won the UEFA Club Footballer of the Year award while playing for Real Madrid:

- Fernando Redondo – 2000
- Zinedine Zidane – 2002

FIFA World Player of the Year

The following players have won the FIFA World Player of the Year award while playing for Real Madrid:

- Luís Figo – 2001
- Ronaldo – 2002
- Zinedine Zidane – 2003

- Fabio Cannavaro – 2006

Internationals

- First international for Spain: Juan Monjardín against Portugal (17 December 1922)
- Most international caps (total): **129** - Luís Figo - Portugal (47 while with the club)
- Most international caps as a Real Madrid player: **111** - Iker Casillas - Spain

Transfers

Highest transfer fees paid

Real Madrid's record signing is Cristiano Ronaldo, who signed for the club from Manchester United for £80 million in July 2009, which also is the world's highest transfer fees. This beat the previous record of £56 million, which the club paid Milan for Kaká in 2009.

	Player	From	Transfer Fee (£ millions)	Date	Ref
1	Cristiano Ronaldo	Manchester United	80	June 2009	
2	Kaká	Milan	56	June 2009	
3	Zinedine Zidane	Juventus	45	July 2001	
4	Luís Figo	Barcelona	37	July 2000	
5	Karim Benzema	Lyon	30	July 2009	
6	Xabi Alonso	Liverpool	30	August 2009	
7	Ronaldo	Internazionale	28	September 2002	
8	David Beckham	Manchester United	25	July 2003	
9	Nicolas Anelka	Arsenal	23	August 1999	
10	Arjen Robben	Chelsea	21	August 2007	

Highest transfer fees received

The club's record sale came in 1 September 2008 , when they sold Robinho to Manchester City for £32.5 million.

	Player	To	Transfer Fee (£ millions)	Date	Ref
1	Robinho	Manchester City	32.5	September 2008	
2	Nicolas Anelka	Paris Saint-Germain	22	July 2000	
3	Arjen Robben	Bayern Munich	22	August 2009	
4	Michael Owen	Newcastle United	17	September 2005	
5	Claude Makélélé	Chelsea	16	September 2003	
6	Wesley Sneijder	Internazionale	14	August 2009	
7	Klaas-Jan Huntelaar	Milan	13	August 2009	
8	Wálter Samuel	Internazionale	11	August 2005	

Managerial records

See also: List of Real Madrid C.F. managers

- First full–time manager: Arthur Johnson
- Longest–serving manager by time: Miguel Muñoz - 15 years in two spells from February 1959 to April 1959 and from April 1960 to 1974 .
- Longest–serving manager by matches: Miguel Muñoz - 604 matches.

Team records

See also: Football records in Spain

Matches

- First competitive match: v 1–3 Barcelona, Campeonato de Copa de S.M. Alfonso XIII, Semi-final, 19 May 1902
- First La Liga match: v 6–0 Europa , La Liga 1929, 19 February 1929
- First Copa del Rey match: v 1–3 Barcelona, Semi-final, 19 May 1902
- First Copa de la Liga match: v 1–0 Real Sociedad, Quarter final, 19 June 1983
- First Supercopa de España match: v 1–0 Real Sociedad, First leg, 13 October 1982
- First match at Santiago Bernabéu: v 3–1 Belenenses, 14 December 1947

First competitive match at Santiago Bernabéu: v 3–1 Español, La Liga 1947–48, 18 December 1947

- First European Cup match: v 2–0 Servette, European Cup 1955–56, (Round 1 - First leg), 8 September 1955
- First UEFA Champions League match: v 0–1 Ajax, Champions League 1995–96, (Group stage), 13 September 1995 real madrid won the champions league 20 consecutive times.
- First UEFA Cup match: v 2–1 Basel, UEFA Cup 1971–72, (Round 1 - First leg), 15 September 1971
- First UEFA Cup Winners' Cup match: v 0–0 Hibernians F.C., Cup Winners' Cup 1970–71, (Round 1 - First leg), 17 September 1970
- First UEFA Super Cup match: v 0–1 Chelsea, 1998 UEFA Super Cup, 28 August 1998
- First Intercontinental Cup match: v 0–0 Peñarol, First leg, 3 July 1960
- First FIFA Club World Cup match: v 3–1 Al-Nassr, 2000 Club World Championship, Group stage, 5 January 2000
- First Latin Cup match: v 2–0 Belenenses, Latin Cup, Semi-final, 22 May 1955
- First Pequeña Copa del Mundo de Clubes match: v 3–2 La Salle, 13 July 1952

Record wins

- Record win: **11-1** against FC Barcelona (during the 1942-43 Copa del Rey)
- Record League win: **11-2** against Elche (during the 1959-60 season).
- Record Cup win: **11-1** against FC Barcelona (during the 1942-43 Copa del Rey)
- Record European win: **9-0** against B 1909 in the 1961–62 European Cup.
- Record home win: **11-1** against FC Barcelona (during the 1942-43 Copa del Rey)
- Record away win:

  1-8 against Real Zaragoza (during the 1987-88 season).

  0-7 against FC Progrès Niedercorn (during the 1978–79 European Cup).

Record defeats

- Record defeat: **1-8** against Espanyol in the 1929-30 season.
- Record League defeat: **1-8** against Espanyol in the 1929-30 season.
- Record Cup defeat: -
- Record European defeat: **5-0** against Milan the 1988-89 season.
- Record home defeat: **0-6** against Athletic Club in the 1930-31 season.
- Record away defeat: **1-8** against Espanyol in the 1929-30 season.

Streaks

- Longest unbeaten run (all major competitions): -
- Longest unbeaten run (League): **31 matches** (from day 36 1987-88 season, to day 28 1988-89 season)
- Longest unbeaten home run (League): **121 matches** (from 1956-57 season, to 1964-65 season)
- Longest winning streak (League): **15 matches** (season 1960-61)
- Longest losing streak (League): -
- Longest drawing streak (League): -
- Longest streak without a win (League): -
- Longest scoring run (League): -
- Longest non-scoring run (League): -
- Longest streak without conceding a goal (League): -

Wins/draws/losses in a season

- Most league wins in a season: **31** in 38 games (during the 2009–10 season).
- Most league home wins in a season: **18** in 19 games (during 1987–88 and 2009–10 seasons).
- Most league away wins in a season: **13** in 19 games (during the 2009–10 season).
- Most league draws in a season: **15** in 34 games (during the 1978–79 season).
- Most league defeats in a season: **13** in 34 games (during the 1973–74 season).
- Fewest league wins in a season: **7** in 18 games (during the 1929–30 season).
- Fewest league draws in a season:
  - **1** in 18 games (during the 1928–29 season).
  - **1** in 22 games (during the 1934–35 and 1939–40 seasons).
- Fewest league defeats in a season: **0** in 18 games (during the 1930–31 season).

Goals

- Most League goals scored in a season: **107** (during the 1989-90 season).
- Fewest League goals scored in a season: **24** (during the 1930-31 season).
- Most League goals conceded in a season: **71** (during the 1950-51 season).
- Fewest League goals conceded in a season: **15** (during the 1931-32 season).

Points

- Most points in a season:

  Two points for a win: **66** in 44 matches (during the 1986-87 season).

  Three points for a win: **96** in 38 matches (during the 2009-10 season).

- Fewest points in a season:

  Two points for a win: **17** in 18 matches (during the 1929-30 season).

  Three points for a win: **70** in 42 matches (during the 1995-96 season).

Season-by-season performance

Main article: List of Real Madrid C.F. seasons

Footnotes

A. The "Other" column constitutes goals and appearances in the Supercopa de España, the Copa de la Liga, the Intercontinental Cup and the FIFA Club World Championship.

Forbes' list of the most valuable football clubs

This is a list of the **richest football clubs** in the world as ranked by *Forbes* magazine on their worth in United States dollars.

2010 rankings

Rankings as of April 2010.

Rank	Team	Country	Value ($M)	Debt as % of value	% change on year	Revenue ($M)	Operating income ($m)
1	Manchester United	England	1,835	46	-2	459	150
2	Real Madrid	Spain	1,323	54	-2	563	130
3	Arsenal	England	1,181	41	-2	369	102
4	Barcelona	Spain	1,000	0	4	513	113
5	Bayern Munich	Germany	990	14	-11	406	61
6	Liverpool	England	822	47	-19	304	37

7	Milan	Italy	800	0	-19	276	41
8	Juventus	Italy	656	3	9	285	57
9	Chelsea	England	646	8	-19	340	-73
10	Internazionale	Italy	413	0	12	276	-14
11	Schalke	Germany	384	50	-25	175	-7
12	Tottenham Hotspur	England	372	29	-16	186	35
13	Lyon	France	333	10	-21	196	5
14	Hamburg	Germany	329	0	0	206	41
15	Roma	Italy	308	0	-19	205	25
16	Werder Bremen	Germany	274	0	-6	161	24
17	Marseille	France	262	0	9	187	19
18	Borussia Dortmund	Germany	261	32	-20	145	8
19	Manchester City	England	258	0	-17	143	-56
20	Newcastle United	England	198	8	-30	142	-49

2009 rankings

Rankings as of April 2009.

Rank	**Team**	**Country**	**Value ($M)**	**Debt as % of value**	**% change on year**	**Revenue ($M)**	**Operating income ($m)**
1	Manchester United	England	1,870	54	4	512	160
2	Real Madrid	Spain	1,353	23	5	576	81
3	Arsenal	England	1,200	107	0	349	80
4	Bayern Munich	Germany	1,110	0	21	465	59
5	Liverpool	England	1,010	59	-4	332	50
6	Milan	Italy	990	0	24	330	58
7	Barcelona	Spain	960	7	22	487	108
8	Chelsea	England	800	92	5	424	-13
9	Juventus	Italy	600	5	18	264	46
10	Schalke	Germany	510	38	9	234	41
11	Tottenham Hotspur	England	445	29	12	228	70

12	Lyon	France	423	18	4	245	94
13	Roma	Italy	381	9	-12	276	69
14	Internazionale	Italy	370	77	-8	272	27
15	Hamburg	Germany	330	0	13	202	44
16	Borussia Dortmund	Germany	325	33	1	183	9
17	Manchester City	England	310	0	62	164	-16
18	Werder Bremen	Germany	292	0	12	177	27
19	Newcastle United	England	285	96	-5	198	-13
20	Stuttgart	Germany	264	0	*not reported*	176	18
21	Aston Villa	England	240	10	26	150	1
21	Marseille	France	240	0	28	200	20
23	Celtic	Scotland	218	14	-4	145	11
24	Everton	England	207	49	5	151	14
25	Rangers	Scotland	194	86	*not reported*	128	15

2008 rankings

This is the April 2008 list as ranked by *Forbes* magazine on their worth in United States dollars.

Rank	Team	Country	Value ($M)	Debt as % of value	% change on year	Revenue ($M)	Operating income($m)
1	Manchester United	England	1,800	60	24	394	111
2	Real Madrid	Spain	1,285	27	24	474	112
3	Arsenal	England	1,200	43	31	329	77
4	Liverpool	England	1,050	65	131	269	60
5	Bayern Munich	Germany	917	0	9	302	72
6	Milan	Italy	798	0	-3	307	54
7	Barcelona	Spain	784	7	47	392	92
8	Chelsea	England	764	0	42	382	-5
9	Juventus	Italy	510	5	-10	196	35
10	Schalke	Germany	470	48	0	154	36
11	Roma	Italy	434	12	94	213	48

12	Tottenham Hotspur	England	414	15	70	207	64
13	Lyon	France	408	7	19	190	15
14	Internazionale	Italy	403	0	-27	207	21
15	Borussia Dortmund	Germany	323	57	63	122	31
16	Newcastle United	England	300	43	16	175	12
17	Hamburg	Germany	293	0	32	163	41
18	Werder Bremen	Germany	262	0	n/a	131	11
19	Valencia	Spain	254	159	31	145	-45
20	Celtic	Scotland	227	11	23	151	48
21	Everton	England	197	30	24	103	-1
22	West Ham United	England	195	23	25	115	-22
23	Manchester City	England	191	63	-8	114	27
24	Aston Villa	England	190	12	36	106	-40
25	Marseille	France	187	0	19	134	13

- Manchester United increased from $1.2 billion to $1.8 billion still remaining at top. While Real Madrid remains second due to an increase of $400 million. Arsenal also remain third after an approximate increase of $350 million.

2007 rankings

This is the March 2007 list as ranked by *Forbes* magazine on their worth in United States dollars.

#	Team	Country	Value ($M)	Debt as % of value	% change on year	Revenue ($M)	Operating income($m)
1	Manchester United	England	1,453	84	6	310	92
2	Real Madrid	Spain	1,036	10	2	374	83
3	Arsenal	England	915	53	9	246	20
4	Bayern Munich	Germany	838	0	9	262	62
5	Milan	Italy	824	0	-10	305	46
6	Juventus	Italy	567	17	-18	321	45
7	Internazionale	Italy	555	n/a	10	264	26
8	Chelsea	England	537	28	6	283	-37

9	Barcelona	Spain	535	12	22	331	12
10	Schalke	Germany	471	53	45	157	37
11	Liverpool	England	454	18	28	225	37
12	Lyon	France	343	n/a	65	163	10
13	Newcastle United	England	260	46	-14	159	11
14	Tottenham Hotspur	England	243	0	27	137	9
15	Roma	Italy	224	0	-15	162	53
16	Hamburg	Germany	221	n/a	n/a	130	31
17	Manchester City	England	208	83	-6	114	9
18	Borussia Dortmund	Germany	199	126	61	114	1
19	Ajax	Netherlands	196	0	13	95	9
20	Celtic	Scotland	185	14	18	106	-8
21	Everton	England	165	32	34	107	-15
22	Marseille	France	157	n/a	n/a	105	6
23	West Ham United	England	156	27	n/a	111	6
24	Rangers	Scotland	147	7	32	113	12
25	Aston Villa	England	140	16	16	91	-21

See also

- Deloitte Football Money League
- List of Premier League football club owners

Article Sources and Contributors

Real Madrid C.F. *Source*: http://en.wikipedia.org/?oldid=390297893 *Contributors*: FGaribay

History of Real Madrid C.F. *Source*: http://en.wikipedia.org/?oldid=372984791 *Contributors*: Keegank11

Santiago Bernabéu Stadium *Source*: http://en.wikipedia.org/?oldid=388053900 *Contributors*: 1 anonymous edits

Alfredo di Stéfano Stadium *Source*: http://en.wikipedia.org/?oldid=388988764 *Contributors*: Keith D

Estadio Chamartín *Source*: http://en.wikipedia.org/?oldid=354696377 *Contributors*:

El Clásico *Source*: http://en.wikipedia.org/?oldid=390503353 *Contributors*: Jotamar

El Derbi madrileño *Source*: http://en.wikipedia.org/?oldid=373178466 *Contributors*: ChicosBailBonds

2010–11 Real Madrid C.F. season *Source*: http://en.wikipedia.org/?oldid=390575258 *Contributors*: Xboxandhalo2

List of Real Madrid C.F. players *Source*: http://en.wikipedia.org/?oldid=390510542 *Contributors*: 1 anonymous edits

List of Real Madrid C.F. managers *Source*: http://en.wikipedia.org/?oldid=388416190 *Contributors*: 1 anonymous edits

List of Real Madrid C.F. presidents *Source*: http://en.wikipedia.org/?oldid=386478836 *Contributors*: Hadrianos1990

List of Real Madrid C.F. records and statistics *Source*: http://en.wikipedia.org/?oldid=388118386 *Contributors*: KSA13

Forbes' list of the most valuable football clubs *Source*: http://en.wikipedia.org/?oldid=389089685 *Contributors*: 1 anonymous edits

Image Sources, Licenses and Contributors

File:Real2007.jpg *Source*: http://bibliocm.bibliolabs.com/mwAnon/index.php?title=File:Real2007.jpg *License*: unknown *Contributors*: -

File:Raul Gonzalez 10mar2007.jpg *Source*: http://bibliocm.bibliolabs.com/mwAnon/index.php?title=File:Raul_Gonzalez_10mar2007.jpg *License*: unknown *Contributors*: -

File:Flag of Spain.svg *Source*: http://bibliocm.bibliolabs.com/mwAnon/index.php?title=File:Flag_of_Spain.svg *License*: unknown *Contributors*: -

File:Flag of France.svg *Source*: http://bibliocm.bibliolabs.com/mwAnon/index.php?title=File:Flag_of_France.svg *License*: unknown *Contributors*: -

File:Flag of Poland.svg *Source*: http://bibliocm.bibliolabs.com/mwAnon/index.php?title=File:Flag_of_Poland.svg *License*: unknown *Contributors*: -

File:Flag of the Netherlands.svg *Source*: http://bibliocm.bibliolabs.com/mwAnon/index.php?title=File:Flag_of_the_Netherlands.svg *License*: unknown *Contributors*: -

File:Florentino perez.jpg *Source*: http://bibliocm.bibliolabs.com/mwAnon/index.php?title=File:Florentino_perez.jpg *License*: unknown *Contributors*: -

Image:MFC 1905 06.jpg *Source*: http://bibliocm.bibliolabs.com/mwAnon/index.php?title=File:MFC_1905_06.jpg *License*: unknown *Contributors*: -

File:Santiagobernabeupanoramav3.jpg *Source*: http://bibliocm.bibliolabs.com/mwAnon/index.php?title=File:Santiagobernabeupanoramav3.jpg *License*: unknown *Contributors*: -

Image:commons-logo.svg *Source*: http://bibliocm.bibliolabs.com/mwAnon/index.php?title=File:Commons-logo.svg *License*: unknown *Contributors*: -

File:Luis Figo 2009 2.jpg *Source*: http://bibliocm.bibliolabs.com/mwAnon/index.php?title=File:Luis_Figo_2009_2.jpg *License*: Creative Commons Attribution 2.5 *Contributors*: User:Sandman888

File:Flag of Hungary.svg *Source*: http://bibliocm.bibliolabs.com/mwAnon/index.php?title=File:Flag_of_Hungary.svg *License*: unknown *Contributors*: -

File:Flag of Chile.svg *Source*: http://bibliocm.bibliolabs.com/mwAnon/index.php?title=File:Flag_of_Chile.svg *License*: unknown *Contributors*: -

File:Flag of Paraguay.svg *Source*: http://bibliocm.bibliolabs.com/mwAnon/index.php?title=File:Flag_of_Paraguay.svg *License*: unknown *Contributors*: -

File:Flag of England.svg *Source*: http://bibliocm.bibliolabs.com/mwAnon/index.php?title=File:Flag_of_England.svg *License*: unknown *Contributors*: -

File:Flag of Romania.svg *Source*: http://bibliocm.bibliolabs.com/mwAnon/index.php?title=File:Flag_of_Romania.svg *License*: unknown *Contributors*: -

File:Flag of Denmark.svg *Source*: http://bibliocm.bibliolabs.com/mwAnon/index.php?title=File:Flag_of_Denmark.svg *License*: unknown *Contributors*: -

File:Flag of Cameroon.svg *Source*: http://bibliocm.bibliolabs.com/mwAnon/index.php?title=File:Flag_of_Cameroon.svg *License*: unknown *Contributors*: -

File:Flag of Turkey.svg *Source*: http://bibliocm.bibliolabs.com/mwAnon/index.php?title=File:Flag_of_Turkey.svg *License*: unknown *Contributors*: -

Image:Soccerball shade.svg *Source*: http://bibliocm.bibliolabs.com/mwAnon/index.php?title=File:Soccerball_shade.svg *License*: unknown *Contributors*: -

File:Injury icon 2.svg *Source*: http://bibliocm.bibliolabs.com/mwAnon/index.php?title=File:Injury_icon_2.svg *License*: unknown *Contributors*: -

Image:Yellow card.svg *Source*: http://bibliocm.bibliolabs.com/mwAnon/index.php?title=File:Yellow_card.svg *License*: unknown *Contributors*: -

Image:Red card.svg *Source*: http://bibliocm.bibliolabs.com/mwAnon/index.php?title=File:Red_card.svg *License*: unknown *Contributors*: -

Image:Soccer Field Transparant.svg *Source*: http://bibliocm.bibliolabs.com/mwAnon/index.php?title=File:Soccer_Field_Transparant.svg *License*: unknown *Contributors*: -

File:GreenButton RightArrow.svg *Source*: http://bibliocm.bibliolabs.com/mwAnon/index.php?title=File:GreenButton_RightArrow.svg *License*: unknown *Contributors*: -

File:Flag placeholder.svg *Source*: http://bibliocm.bibliolabs.com/mwAnon/index.php?title=File:Flag_placeholder.svg *License*: unknown *Contributors*: -

File:Flag of Uruguay.svg *Source*: http://bibliocm.bibliolabs.com/mwAnon/index.php?title=File:Flag_of_Uruguay.svg *License*: unknown *Contributors*: -

File:Alfredo di stefano1947.jpg *Source*: http://bibliocm.bibliolabs.com/mwAnon/index.php?title=File:Alfredo_di_stefano1947.jpg *License*: unknown *Contributors*: -

File:HugoSanchez.JPG *Source*: http://bibliocm.bibliolabs.com/mwAnon/index.php?title=File:HugoSanchez.JPG *License*: unknown *Contributors*: -

File:IkerCasillas.JPG *Source*: http://bibliocm.bibliolabs.com/mwAnon/index.php?title=File:IkerCasillas.JPG *License*: unknown *Contributors*: -

File:Flag of Montenegro.svg *Source*: http://bibliocm.bibliolabs.com/mwAnon/index.php?title=File:Flag_of_Montenegro.svg *License*: unknown *Contributors*: -

File:Flag of SFR Yugoslavia.svg *Source*: http://bibliocm.bibliolabs.com/mwAnon/index.php?title=File:Flag_of_SFR_Yugoslavia.svg *License*: unknown *Contributors*: -

File:Flag of Wales 2.svg *Source*: http://bibliocm.bibliolabs.com/mwAnon/index.php?title=File:Flag_of_Wales_2.svg *License*: unknown *Contributors*: -

File:Flag of Spain (1785-1873 and 1875-1931).svg *Source*: http://bibliocm.bibliolabs.com/mwAnon/index.php?title=File:Flag_of_Spain_(1785-1873_and_1875-1931).svg *License*: unknown *Contributors*: -

File:Flag of Spain under Franco 1938 1945.svg *Source*: http://bibliocm.bibliolabs.com/mwAnon/index.php?title=File:Flag_of_Spain_under_Franco_1938_1945.svg *License*: unknown *Contributors*: -

File:Flag of Spain 1945 1977.svg *Source*: http://bibliocm.bibliolabs.com/mwAnon/index.php?title=File:Flag_of_Spain_1945_1977.svg *License*: unknown *Contributors*: -

CPSIA information can be obtained at www.ICGtesting.com
Printed in the USA
BVOW050300171212
308397BV00003B/55/P

9 781241 147228